The Flight of the Red Knot

The Flight of the Red Knot

A natural history account of a small bird's
annual migration from the Arctic Circle to the
tip of South America and back

by Brian Harrington
with Charles Flowers

W. W. Norton & Company
New York · London

The text of this book is composed in Bembo
Composition by Bytheway Typesetting Services Inc.
Manufacturing by South China Printing Company Ltd.
Book design by Douglass Scott and Tong-Mei Chang/WGBH Design

Library of Congress Cataloging-in-Publication Data

Harrington, Brian
The flight of the red knot: a natural history account of a small bird's annual migration
from the Arctic Circle to the tip of South America and back /Brian Harrington.

p.   cm.
Includes index.
1. Red knot—Migration. 2. Red knot. 3. Red knot—Migration—Pictorial works.
4. Red knot—Pictorial works. I. Title.
QL696.C48H37   1996
598.3'3—dc20   95-7876

ISBN 0-393-03861-0

W. W. Norton & Company, Inc., 500 Fifth Avenue, New York, NY 10110
W. W. Norton & Company, Ltd., 10 Coptic Street, London WC1A 1PU

1 2 3 4 5 6 7 8 9 0

Published in association with WGBH Boston and the Manomet Observatory.

All photography © David C. Twichell except the following: pp. 2, 10–11: © Steven Holt/
VIREO; pp. 27, 79 (bottom): © Arthur Morris/VIREO; pp. 31 (top and bottom), 42–43,
62–63, 79 (top), 90 (bottom), 111 (top), 126–127: © Arthur Morris/BIRDS AS ART; pp.
47, 74 (inset), 103 (bottom): © Clay Myers/The Wildlife Collection; pp. 87 (top and
bottom), 90 (top): © Fred Bruemmer; pp. 66 (bottom), 130 (bottom): © Pablo Canevari;
p. 119: © Cary Wolinsky/Trillium.

Frontispiece:
Red knots swooping in
to the shallows near
Delaware Bay, New
Jersey, in May are
caught in different stages
of the typical landing
pattern: the legs are
lowered as the birds
descend, the tail feathers
fan, and the wings
sweep forward.

CONTENTS

Preface   *6*

INTRODUCTION: Precarious Cycle   *13*

Patagonia and Tierra del Fuego   28
ONE: October through February   *30*

Heading North through Brazil to Delaware Bay   48
TWO: March through April   *52*

The Shores of Delaware Bay   68
THREE: May through June   *70*

The Arctic   80
FOUR: June through August   *84*

Heading South through Canada and the Northeastern U. S.   96
FIVE: August through October   *100*

The Migratory Chain   117
SIX: Into Our Future   *118*

APPENDICES: Important Issues about Shorebirds
Banding   *141*
Diet   *145*
Market Hunting   *148*
Current Threats to Delaware Bay   *152*
Mud   *160*
Navigation   *163*
Migrants in the Midwest: The Cheyenne Bottoms Story   *169*

Notes   *176*

Acknowledgments   *185*

Index   *189*

Preface

I STAND ON A BEACH in southern New Jersey as tens of thousands of birds gather in the middle distance. So many of them have come here together, they are packed so densely, and they are moving continuously in such perfect unison—shifting higher onto the beach whenever the ocean waves roll into shore, descending to feed when the surf recedes—that the flock looks something like a huge feathered quilt, gently flapping in the spring breeze. As it drifts upward and downward, this living fabric also slides backward and forward along the shoreline of Delaware Bay. Its top side is a ruddy brownish black, splashed here and there with calico; on the underside, a rich blend of rust and salmon is broken at intervals with slices of crispest white.

A murmur rises from the quilt when it flutters to the sands, the characteristic sound of this multitude of red knots jabbing individually for the fodder that litters the beach. There must be fifty thousand knots here, almost a third of the entire North American population of the species.

Yet just the week before not one was in the area. A week before that, I caught and banded some of these very birds in southern Brazil, as is evident from the distinctive orange plastic bands visible on their legs now. And a week from now these knots will have reached their breeding grounds a thousand miles north of here in the Canadian tundra. The south Jersey coast, in other words, is only a stopover for the knots on their amazing journey between the southernmost and northernmost

Just before Memorial Day, a mixed flock of red knots, other shorebirds, and laughing gulls are packed together about two hours before afternoon high tide at Reed's Beach, a summer colony on Delaware Bay. Exhausted and hungry after their recent flight from South America, the knots frenetically search exposed areas for food until nightfall, when they commute to the marshes of the Atlantic side to roost.

lands of our hemisphere. Their great feast here allows them to replenish the fuel they need to continue the next leg. Many have come here from as far away as Tierra del Fuego, perhaps stopping only once along the way. This scarcely credible journey is shared with other so-called shorebirds, a term ornithologists use to describe plovers, sandpipers, and their allies.

The spectacle of this spring shorebird migration at Delaware Bay is thrilling, mysterious for anyone lucky enough to experience it. But it also raises serious questions of species survival and our responsibility to our fellow creatures. What would happen if this beach, whether by human accident or by design, were lost to the exhausted, traveling red knots? Is sufficient food available anywhere else within striking distance of their arctic nesting places?

This book explores those questions by bringing together what researchers have discovered about the red knots' annual migration: a story of marathon flights connecting widely scattered points that provide abundant food resources, but only in season.

My interest in the red knot, indeed my continuing chronic interest in all birds, goes back to my teens spent near the Sakonnet River on the Rhode Island coast in the early 1950s. The first stage, alas, involved my prowling around the twenty acres of land behind the family house, armed with a BB gun. Nothing, not even the first sparrows singing in spring, was safe from the intrepid, unrepentant hunter.

Then one early morning in September, in the calm after the dying of a nor'easter, I was sneaking along a stone wall, stalking our neighbor's herd of dairy cows (owing to my foolishness, they were probably not yielding much milk that summer). Suddenly I came across a flock of fifteen or twenty birds unlike any I had ever seen before. In their posture and worm-hunting behavior, they resembled red-breasted robins, but they had jet black undersides and a topside flecked with gold, blacks, and browns. A distinct white line stretched across the side of the head from forehead to nape.

Switching my sights to this tempting new quarry, which seemed like easy pickings, I crawled nearer. Far more alert than the cows, they had obviously spotted me long before I drew very close. The entire group rose up in an amazingly rapid flight, described a huge circle in a tight flock that held perfect formation, and then landed in the corner of the field farthest away from me. Annoyed, I spent the rest of the morning trying to get close; fortunately for them, their wariness completely frustrated my designs.

That night I looked up golden plovers in a book my grandmother had given me. I learned about the concept of migration, about how this particular migrant traveled all the way from the Arctic to Argentina. I also was introduced to its cousin, the very similar-looking black-bellied plover, which is the more common of the two in Rhode Island. The second stage of my fascination with birds began at dawn the very next morning when I returned to the field, this time armed with my brother's telescope. Close inspection confirmed that I had indeed happened upon a flock of golden plovers—and I was hooked on the challenge of finding and identifying bird species. Shorebirds on the beach and in the pastures lying near the Sakonnet quickly became my favorite prey in this new form of hunting. Before long I was restless for a greater variety of species and pestered parents or bird-watching friends to take me to adjacent states where there were a greater assortment and larger numbers of shorebirds.

It seemed only natural that, little more than a decade later, I was studying nesting seabirds at Johnston Atoll in the Central Pacific. A single island in the atoll was the only breeding spot available to seabirds within at least three hundred thousand square miles of ocean. Loss of this haven would devastate these populations. This disturbing truth stayed with me when I returned to work on shorebirds in Massachusetts. Even as an adolescent warming to the study, I had recognized that not all coastline is equal in the eyes of shorebirds: quite clearly, some relatively small sections of coast are used by very high proportions of entire species populations. Whether Johnston Atoll or a certain stretch of beach in the Northeast, there are special places where bird watchers go to see shorebirds. To shorebirds these very same spots are critical links in hemispheric chains of migration.

Adult red knots develop their brightest plumage in preparation for the breeding season, the only time when back feathers become russet. Warily alert, perhaps because of the photographer, they are characteristically spaced in a kind of beehive pattern, packed together as closely as possible while leaving enough room to spread their wings and take off instantly.

Precarious Cycle

*T*HE LEGS OF THE RED KNOT'S amazing journey can be likened to crossing a stream on a chain of natural stepping-stones—some relatively close together, others so widely spaced that it is necessary to take almost inconceivably gigantic strides. For the moment even those of us who most avidly follow the knots on their vast circuit can only guess at the likely consequences of their losing any of these strategic footholds. Indeed, the single most startling discovery to emerge from systematic observation of the red knot is the small number of migration-staging areas where feeding, or "refueling," takes place.

Yet the knot is only one of the 177 species of shorebirds found around the globe that are vitally dependent on such stepping-stones during migratory journeys. Dozens of kinds of sandpipers and plovers wing between the extremes of all of the continents, except perhaps Antarctica. Like the knot, many of them perform incredible epic flights, whether tiny sandpipers barely larger than sparrows or curlews the size of crows.

In our hemisphere millions of arctic-breeding shorebirds that migrate between North and South America need their traditional stopovers on the coastal and inland wetlands of the United States for acquiring fat to fuel flight legs that are thousands of miles long. Of the thirty-five species common to North America, many concentrate at a small number of essential, irreplaceable wetlands where easily retrievable food is found in high density. Since up to 80 percent of a species will stop at a specific site every year, the perfect combination of resources is obviously rare.

14

Like many shorebirds, knots depend upon the food resources of coastal beaches and tidal flats for their survival. These knots with their drab winter plumage are an unusual group that stays on the beaches of west Florida in October through May rather than make the breed's customary southward migration to Patagonia.

Nevertheless, we have not yet found simple answers to why shorebirds will favor a particular site, nor have we been able to predict what impact the loss of such critical sites might have. Complex geological and biological processes, little understood in their own right, are involved in studying the problem.

Nevertheless, numerous clues do suggest that shorebirds are perilously dependent for survival on their traditional layovers. For example, all of the major Atlantic staging areas share two evidently essential characteristics: extensive intertidal flats and places where birds can rest during high tides. Such a combination of resources often occurs at beaches close to coastal inlets, large river mouths, or large bays. The flats, whether formed by the movement of tides, ocean currents, or rivers, typically have high mud content, as in Canada's James Bay and Bay of Fundy. Moreover, almost all of the coastal sites lie at estuaries, where the mixing of fresh and salt water promotes some of the highest known levels of biological productivity. By contrast, relatively few shorebirds pause to feed at ocean beaches, rocky coastlines, coastal ponds, isolated salt marshes, or large bays that have only a few mud flats.

Preservation of wetlands, then, has become the first line of battle for maintaining the traditional foraging grounds of migratory shorebirds which are now threatened, from the vast Pantanal region in Brazil to the mangrove systems of Suriname to the smaller marshes like Cheyenne Bottoms in Kansas. The general term *wetlands* includes such marshes and small isolated streams, along with the large estuaries and coastal lagoons. All are vitally important to maintaining biodiversity because they serve as genetic resource banks for unique life forms: that is to say, the isolation of the wetlands combines with the poor mobility, or "habitat imprisonment," of their denizens to produce genetic isolation as well. As a result, the evolution of species in wetlands often produces unique life forms.

In addition, marine wetlands are especially important because they produce extremely rich food webs that serve as "energy engines" for a high proportion of ocean creatures. For example, many coastal and marine fish travel long distances to lay their eggs in marshes, bays, mangrove swamps, and rivers, where their fry will feast during their hazardous larval development. Finally, many bird species—not only shorebirds but also ducks, geese, swans, and rails—also depend on the wetland systems for nutritive resources.

Yet more than half the wetlands in the lower forty-eight of the United States have been destroyed since the coming of Europeans, including more than 90 percent of wetlands in such major bird-flyway states as California, Missouri, and Iowa. Still remaining, according to the Office of Technology Assessment, are roughly ninety million acres, 95 percent of them inland and the rest coastal or estuarine. In spite of government regulations, these existing wetlands are being converted at an increasing rate for construction, commerce, agriculture, and recreation—with the inevitable consequences for shorebirds. The only good news, and it is a slender thread, is that coastal areas are being destroyed at a slower pace than those inland.

Customarily we think of a species as endangered when its population has already been drastically reduced to only a few individuals, as with the whooping crane or the Siberian tiger. For birds like the red knot, however, the scenario for serious trouble follows a different script. The challenge is not to preserve a dwindling number of survivors but to protect those few pinpoints on the earth that are crucial to the continued existence of hundreds of thousands of birds, perhaps entire populations. If an oil spill radically diminished the rich food resources at strategic haunts along the Patagonian coastline or if commercial development devastated key North American sites, essential links in a unique chain would be broken. Hemispheric shorebird populations would be annihilated.

When discussing animal conservation, we usually have precise numbers for the populations of endangered species; by definition, their numbers have dropped to the point where all individuals can all too easily be counted. In this book, however, we are instead concerned with preventing a group of relatively common birds from declining to that point. Because most kinds of shorebirds still have healthy populations, it is not

Before the era of recreational vehicles and sailboats light enough to be pulled ashore, tens of thousands of shorebirds annually stopped at this beach to rest and refuel at peak migration. Now, perhaps only a couple of thousand brave the crowds of human intruders.

simple to count them. For example, it took me eight years of work to arrive at a working estimate of the red knot population in North America. The birds were marked during migration, then recaptured in later years as I worked on projects in Argentina, Brazil, Venezuela, Texas, Florida, Delaware Bay, James Bay, and Massachusetts. But even this substantial amount of work, combined with reports from some six hundred contacts throughout the hemisphere, has not yet yielded a very precise estimate: i.e., 250,000 plus or minus 100,000 birds. Still, it is better than current estimates for any other nonendangered shorebirds.

Another method is to count a shorebird species during breeding or wintering seasons, a practical approach, since shorebirds live in places where they are quite visible. On the other hand, most North American shorebirds winter in remote areas of South America and typically disperse themselves over vast stretches of coastline. This has not deterred intrepid biologists like Guy Morrison of the Canadian Wildlife Service from flying over these enormous areas at low altitude in order to count shorebirds and map key wintering areas. Still, too many factors militate against accuracy in such censusing: wind conditions, tidal rhythms, and clouds.

Breeding areas are no more reliable for counting populations, because most shorebirds nest in remote arctic tundra where they are secretive and difficult to find, due to their cryptic coloration. Some studies have successfully determined accurate densities at specific sites, but we know that such densities are highly variable from place to place—or even in the same location from year to year. Consequently, a census at one time or place tells us very little about numbers elsewhere.

With shorebirds, perhaps the best opportunity for estimating populations occurs during migration, when so many of them characteristically funnel down from the Arctic through strategic migration areas before fanning out again into dispersed wintering grounds. On the other hand, there are obstacles. While we can count the number of individuals present at any one time, we cannot readily tell which of those here today will not be gone tomorrow. The idea of marking birds in order to determine turnover rates sounds simple enough, but actually catching enough birds and then searching through teeming flocks on successive days in order to relocate them can be tedious and eventually unrewarding.

It is possible, however, to mark birds, then later record how many marked birds are found for each one hundred or one thousand birds captured. Using simple algebra and the ratio of marked to unmarked birds, we can compile an estimate of the population size. Certain assumptions are involved in the method, but if they can be verified within reason, the results will be useful.

For our working estimates of the American knot population, we have used these marked-to-unmarked bird-resighting ratios, as well as the censuses taken at wintering and migration-staging areas. Both methods have produced roughly the same estimate, somewhere between one hundred thousand and two hundred thousand birds. This seems a huge number, if you imagine sitting on a beach and counting the individuals one by one. Compared with human population figures, however, it would be equivalent to relatively small cities like Raleigh, North Carolina, Madison, Wisconsin, or Lubbock, Texas.

To take another example, one of the most common shorebirds in North America is the semipalmated sandpiper, but Guy Morrison of the Canadian Wildlife Service found only about 1.9 million of these tiny birds in a census in their wintering range in South America. That is about the number of humans who live in New York City's borough of Queens.

The point, in both instances, is that the populations of even the most common shorebirds in North America—and indeed, the rest of the world—are not large. This insight, combined with the recognition that high proportions of these populations may use a single staging or wintering area, underlies the focus on conservation in this book.

Effective preservation programs, we have learned, can be built only upon foundations of solid, thorough research. We at the Manomet Observatory have been working since the 1970s to develop a comprehensive strategy for protecting the amazing migration systems of shorebirds. In the last few years our work has begun to bear fruit in ways we

Volunteers capture red knots for identification marking at Reed's Beach. A "rocket net" is anchored at one end of the landward side of the beach, then five yard-long rockets attached to the opposite side are fired toward the water, dropping the web in place. The yellow-and-white cotton cover is gently placed over the struggling birds, who become calm when they can't see the sky. Perhaps thirty to forty birds will be kept briefly in each of the cardboard boxes, evidently more contented when they are grouped together tightly.

Page 26, Top:
Flexible plastic bands in
different colors are arranged
in identification patterns
on both legs of a marked
bird. A metal band with a
unique eight-digit tracking
number is attached to the
upper right leg and, for
easier spotting, covered
with the bright-blue
waterproof tape seen here
in the upper right corner.

Page 26, Bottom:
Yellow picric acid dye,
harmless to birds, is
swabbed on selected red
knots in Argentina in
April. The dye will last
until the birds grow new
feathers in mid-summer,
helping observers along the
northward migratory route
pick out banded specimens
in a huge flock.

could only have hoped for when we started. On the one hand, we have a much better idea of the timing and scope of the migration systems; on the other, we have participated in planting the seeds of conservation strategies and worked along with policymakers in and out of government in North and South America who have initiated strategic international planning.

Such promising developments would have been impossible without bird counts, migration data, and species-specific studies. For that reason, we founded the International Shorebird Survey (ISS), a volunteer-operated program to assemble the facts needed for recognition and protection of strategic wetlands, for better understanding of migration itself, and for monitoring population trends in animals known to be especially vulnerable to site destruction. A major goal was to learn whether shorebirds tend to concentrate at migration sites to such a degree that they will be imperiled by the loss of key staging areas.

Without the enthusiastic, skilled efforts of the ISS volunteers, the costs of collecting this kind of information would have been prohibitive. During the group's first fifteen years of operation, over six hundred people were able to gather useful data from more than five hundred locations in thirty-eight states and from more than one hundred sites in thirty-five countries south of the United States—a remarkable survey of shorebird migration covering North, Central, and South America. Each participant offered to take a census of a designated area at least once every ten days during a migration season; most have been able to repeat this annual census for years on end.

The results prove that a piecemeal approach to conservation will not work. It turns out to be just as important to document the varying energy needs of different bird species, for instance, as it is to document the role played by specific stopover sites. At the same time, marking the birds with bands can provide information on population status, migration patterns, and location of critical staging areas, while it also enables us to detect where new problems may be developing. The combination of data is necessary to lead us to a better understanding of just how shorebirds actually complete their extraordinary migration and how each factor is essential in maintaining the migratory system.

Based upon the work of ISS, we now know that most migratory shorebirds of the Western Hemisphere seem to depend on such strategic stopover sites as Delaware Bay, Cheyenne Bottoms in Kansas, and Lagoa do Peixe in Brazil. Building upon that finding, we need to identify passage zones, flight timing, and still more staging areas as an important next step in setting objectives for the conservation and management of the most important sites. But the ISS not only accumulates raw data; in a less tangible way, it also establishes channels of communication that promote the rapid and effective growth of new programs like the Western Hemisphere Shorebird Reserve Network (WHSRN), a system of protection for stopover sites. And the ripple effect continues: from WHSRN has grown an even larger program, Wetlands for the Americas (WA).

The hard work of the dedicated ISS volunteers informs and inspires much of this book about the red knot, its annual journey, and the key sites of shorebird migration in the Western Hemisphere. Along with these volunteers and professionals in the field, I hope not only to stimulate the interest of bird watchers and natural historians but also to win the understanding and support of land managers, developers, governmental planners, and elected officials—i.e., those who could use their power to reverse the effects of habitat loss on shorebirds.

This book is dedicated to that possibility.

Page 27:
The green tab on the red knot's right leg is not one of the bands that identify a specific individual bird (like the red and yellow bands), but a marker that is part of an internationally coordinated color scheme to show where birds are captured and banded. Green, for example, indicates that this bird was tagged in the United States.

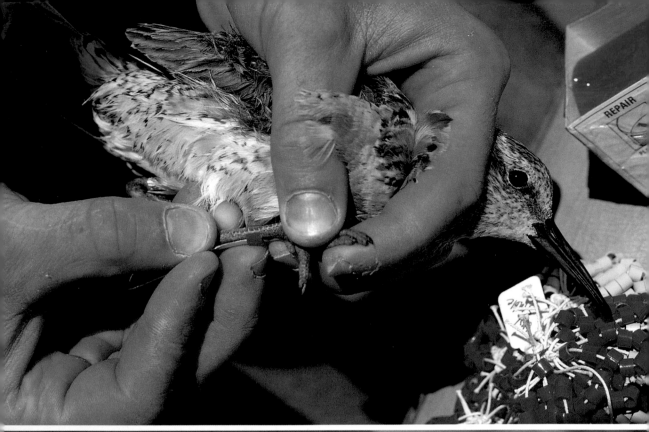

Patagonia and Tierra del Fuego

CHILE

PATAGONIA

Peninsula Valdez

Bahia Bustamente

Golfo San Jorge

ARGENTINA

Strait of Magellan

Bahia Lomas

Falkland Islands

Bahia San Sebastian

Tierra del Fuego

Punta Popper

Rio Grande

NORTH AMERICA

North Atlantic Ocean

Caribbean Sea

Pacific Ocean

SOUTH AMERICA

South Atlantic Ocean

CHAPTER ONE

October through February

In spring plumage, the red knot exhibits a distinctive red band over the eye, reddish feathers sprinkled over the back, and a brick-red breast. Males tend to be brighter in color, but the distinction is slight. This bird, trolling for horseshoe crab eggs floating in the water, could be of either sex.

The new winter plumage of this red knot is pristine. The light-colored edges of the feathers will wear off very quickly, and the back and wing feathers will be noticeably frayed and broken within a couple of months. The comparatively long bill may indicate that this bird is female.

THE RACE OF AMERICAN sandpipers known to us as red knots, or *Calidris canutus rufa*, is the largest of the beach sandpipers. The average specimen is approximately ten-and-one-half inches long with wings that open to a span of twenty to twenty-one inches. Its normal cry is a low two-note whistle, variously described as "whit-whit" or "wahquoit," occasionally varied with the churring "knut" sound that inspired the bird's name. As is typical of sandpipers, its straight, dark bill is sturdy yet pliable. In the spring, when these birds initiate their annual migratory flight from their wintering places at the tip of South America toward breeding grounds in the Arctic, they are at their most colorful. The edges of the head, underside of the neck, and under-parts are a unique brownish red, sometimes described as salmon colored, that grades to a dull white below the tail, or an even paler shade in the female. The upper body is dark brown, with streaks of reddish brown, tan, and black, while the tail is uniformly brownish gray, whitening around the edges. Legs and feet are a dull yellow green. Months later the North American autumn brings a change in coloration as old feathers fade and new ones are grown: the body becomes ashen gray and white, with black and off-white at the margins of the back feathers and faint dusky markings below; the rump and base of the tail become a dull white.

Other races of knots occupy breeding ranges that stretch to the most northerly limits of land in both the Old and New worlds, migrating to wintering grounds as far south as Australia, New Zealand, and

South Africa. These spectacular migrations have attracted a great deal of study over the past two decades, taking researchers to the ends of the earth to discover the birds' secrets. No single species of shorebird, or *wader*, to use the European term, can perfectly represent shorebirds in general, but our American red knot's known life cycle embodies the feeding, social, and migratory habits of the winged globe-trotters who travel the farthest every year.

The knots return every fall to their favored wintering spots along the coasts of Patagonia and Tierra del Fuego, where they are perfectly at home from October through February, the months of the southern hemispheric, or austral, spring and summer. This seasonal habitat, which could be termed either summering or wintering grounds according to one's position on the globe, is the southernmost destination of one of nature's longest and most spectacular nomadic circuits.

To most of us in North America or Europe, the tapering Argentine extremity of South America known as Patagonia, along with the great island and archipelago of Tierra del Fuego at its southern tip, has come to represent all that is remote and wild in the world. Even to those Argentines who live in the northern, more developed regions of their country, the vast plain and forests of Patagonia and the windswept moors of Tierra del Fuego are a place apart, evocative of both the rigor and promise of the frontier. Settled by Europeans only within the last century, these are primarily districts of scattered sheep and cattle ranches.

But despite the mystique that Eurocentric thinking ascribes to the region, the truth is that the far southern reaches of South America are no more "antipodal" than any other spot on our planet. In fact, the traditionally used term *migratory* does not satisfactorily describe the situation of the red knot, for it suggests movement between one house and another, between a true home and a summer place. By contrast, the red knot and similar travelers could more accurately be called *nomadic* — and *globally* nomadic, unlike any human beings to whom the term can be applied. To these birds one place is potentially as much a center and focus of life as any other during their year of periodic travels dictated by the seasonal availability of food. Each home is as good as another, for reasons different and yet the same.

Answering the question of why knots travel such a great distance from their arctic breeding grounds to the tip of South America would be an exciting development in our understanding of migration. We have some clues, but they are more suggestive than probative. One major factor may be that the populations of marine worms, clams, mussels, and nutritious small crustaceans in Patagonia and Tierra del Fuego peak from November through January, while similar food resources along the northeastern United States coast peak in July or August, right on schedule for the knot's return from the Arctic. Another factor is surely the lay of the land: for shorebirds like the red knot that forage for food on intertidal flats, few spots can rival Patagonia, where an enormous tidal flux of thirty feet or more creates a vast intertidal zone.

One feature scattered in sections along the Patagonian shoreline from Chubut Province down to Tierra del Fuego is especially seductive to feeding knots. Pitted shelves of *restinga*, a densely packed sediment, are formed from dust swept off the region's treeless plains by the relentless offshore winds. This material stretches out in broad, level intertidal platforms near the low-tide mark, cut intermittently by waves and studded with pools of standing water when the ocean is at ebb. Fishes and other marine creatures survive in these pools until the high tide returns.

Throughout the shelves lie dense beds of mussels along with their young, known as "spat," whose shells are not yet fully formed. Because the *restinga* is not as hard as true rock, the mussels are not able to hold themselves in place with their characteristic iron grip. Although they can successfully resist the pull of waves and tides by clinging with their byssal threads, they are easily pried loose by the ravenous, opportunistic red knots, whose soft sandpiper bills are ill suited for rapidly harvesting mussels from more solid holdfasts. Also, fortuitously for the birds, the semifirm characteristics of the *restinga* allow the red knots to work quickly during low tide, unerringly picking off spat that has grown to just the right bite size during the southern spring and summer.

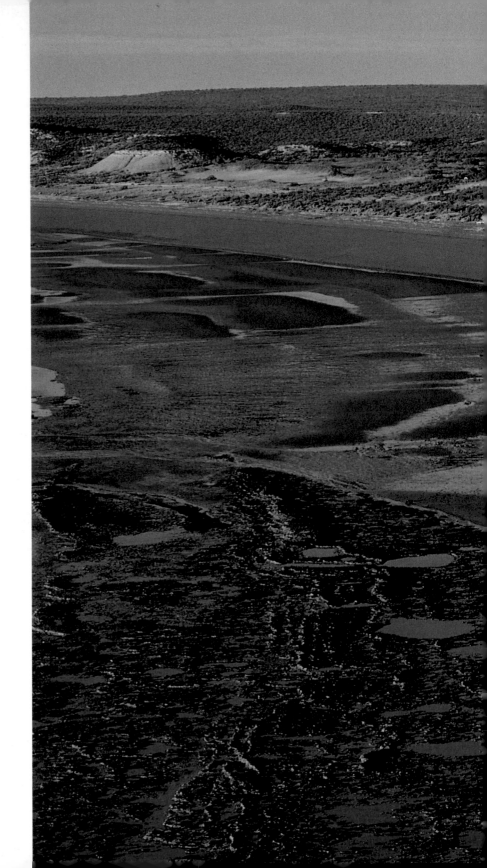

34

Restinga, *the distinctive
sediment seen along much
of the Patagonian coast, is
uncovered at low tide at
Golfo San Jorge,
Argentina, providing the
red knot's favorite feeding
sites from November to
February. Because the
tidal flux is a dramatic
thirty feet or more, whales
will be swimming over this
area at high tide.*

As we discover more about how shorebirds find and retrieve their food, we find over and again that each species has abilities that are specifically tailored to the prey and habitats it prefers. Even a bird's physical features, like legs and bills, have evolved to suit its characteristic foraging pattern.

In this respect, knots are something of a curiosity. Most of their kindred sandpiper species forage largely or wholly by probing with their bills for prey buried in mud, sand, or earth. But during many seasons, knots ferret out their food by sight, as plovers evidently do. Some shorebird species may also hunt their food using smell and taste in addition to vision and touch.[1]

For the knots, bivalves are among the most satisfying of delicacies. The birds' digestive systems have evolved accordingly, becoming exceptionally well suited for processing shellfish. Some other shorebirds find the shells of their prey indigestible and have to regurgitate them in pellets, much as owls cough up hair and bone pellets separated from the edible flesh of the small mammals they hunt. The red knot is more fortunate: when it swallows mussel spat or a surf clam, its gizzard grinds shell along with everything else, and the waste passes through the entire digestive tract.

In sum, *rufa* in its wintering zones is exclusively a bird of the shoreline. Never in all my research travels in the Southern Hemisphere, which have covered the entire length of Argentina, have I found a red knot inland, but I have seen them by the thousands along the coast. One major wintering area is slightly more than a mile north of the small town of Río Grande in Tierra del Fuego. In November and December of 1979, I visited this stretch of Atlantic coast on a World-Wildlife-Fund-sponsored research trip, along with Guy Morrison of the Canadian Wildlife Service. In this one location and an area just south of Punta Popper, we counted more than five thousand birds foraging on mussels at low tide on the outer edges of the *restinga,* or more than 90 percent of the knots we would find during the entire trip. We did not survey Bahia Lomas, a large bay on the south side of the eastern entrance to the Strait of Magellan, because ground access is so difficult.

Six years later Morrison and his coworkers, Ken Ross and Pablo Canevari, were able to study this area by airplane. Amazingly, this 1985 team counted an estimated 41,700 knots, or about one-third my working estimate of the total world population of *rufa*.

Elsewhere on Tierra del Fuego during the 1979 trip, we observed smaller clusters of red knots on the tidal mud flats at Bahia San Sebastian, feeding sporadically on small surf clams. Farther to the north in Patagonia's Chubut Province, the wintering knots along the intertidal mud flats at Bahia Bustamente were favoring half-inch, thin-shelled tellin clams, which they seized by probing in the soft, wet sand. All of our observations affirmed, in other words, that the rich marine resources of the intertidal regions are crucial to the red knot at this time of year.

Yet another felicitous factor is the length of day in the southern hemispheric summer. Because there are more hours of daylight than the twelve at the equator, more low tides occur between dawn and dusk, thus affording the knots increased opportunities for their foraging. Even if food were as abundant along the coasts of the Northern Hemisphere as in the south, the comparatively limited hours of daylight would restrict the knots' feeding time to the fewer low tides. In effect, for the red knot, as for other shorebirds, migration becomes not merely a matter of targeting adequate food supplies but also of stretching the time available in which to harvest them.

During these months of winter foraging, red knots hone one of the most remarkable skills of shorebird species: formation flying. According to one interpretation, a flock of shorebirds is virtually a single organism, its movements coordinated by an amorphous "brain" and "nervous system" that somehow connects each individual bird to all the rest. A flock of five hundred or so knots might assume a globular shape one moment, then distend almost instantaneously into a series of irregular small "clouds" linked by strings of birds rising and falling. No one quite understands the function of these magnificent displays of coordination.

In hopes of finding an explanation, I have closely followed the movements of red knots on and around their feeding areas during my various research visits to Tierra del Fuego. By chance, one of the first flocking displays I ever watched as I stood on the beach nearby remains perhaps the most impressive, an aerial exhibition by knots that had gathered one overcast day at the outer edge of the *restinga* along the shoreline near Rio Grande. Although they had apparently come there to feed, they were extremely flighty and spent little time actually foraging. Again and again huge flocks of three thousand or more would rise up into the air and fly north or south along the coast in a low strung-out pattern, with the lead birds sometimes climbing one hundred to two hundred feet above the water. After ten to fifteen seconds of this maneuver, the birds at the rear of the flock would echo the ascension. This rising movement would ripple through the entire formation in a sinuous curve that reminded me of the snap of a whip. A moment later, all of the knots would plummet in unison toward the surface of the water or the shelves of *restinga* but stop barely three feet overhead and seem to hover in the shape of a giant blanket. Next, again with perfect synchronization, the knots would change direction with a dramatically pronounced flash of white from the thousands of undersides facing me, which would swiftly darken to faint gray as they wheeled, turning their backs. There was yet more shifting of shape as the wonderful display continued, sometimes with the flock joining together in a dense ball that would lift rapidly into the clouded sky. Indeed, the performance lasted for most of the hour I spent there, equally transfixed and puzzled, and I have replayed it over and again in memory, though to little avail, from the scientific rather than the aesthetic perspective. To this day I have not the slightest idea what could have been stimulating these remarkable synchronous flights.

Of course, a certain amount of group aerial motion is normally involved in the passage of red knots back and forth between the *restinga* where they feed, the satellite resting grounds where they preen and rest for an hour or so, and the principal resting sites where they pass the hours between low tides. The birds typically make their move to the

A flock of red knots banks and wheels balletically, descending as one toward a nighttime roosting spot.

Knots in winter plumage foraging on the beach are probing for the small cochina clam, one of their preferred foods. Probing birds may use some little-understood sense of pressure feedback to find the bivalves, which burrow down two to three inches into the sand, almost out of reach of the knot's bill.

latter areas one to two hours before high tide and will remain there, if not disturbed, until two to three hours after the crest. At that point the flock becomes visibly restless, its individual members beginning to shift about and resume their preening. Finally, when the tide has fallen far enough, the knots fly the short distance to the waterline and start hunting for prey again, at first halfheartedly and then with increasing enthusiasm as the tide falls. Although knots do forage day and night at some sites, especially during migration, it is far more common at the wintering grounds for them to leave the beaches when the sun sets and fly to shallow sections of nearby lagoons. There they rest through the night in dense flocks.

The image of commuters doggedly pursuing their daily schedule is more than a little apt. In Argentina in the southern spring of early 1981, when I was working closely with a group of Manomet friends on the shores of Golfo San José at Peninsula Valdez, I felt the need for a little solitude one evening. I strolled down the beach, idly watching the guanacos (members of the camily family related to the larger llamas and alpacas) that grazed on the plateau above our camp. Suddenly, from about a half mile southward down the beach, there was a tremendous, rapidly increasing roar that sounded like an oncoming freight train. As I instinctively ducked, a tight flock of about five hundred knots flew overhead so fast and low that the aggregate noise of wind ripping between their flight feathers was momentarily frightening. Their work done for the day, these birds were headed, "hell-bent for leather," toward the shallow *salitral* (salt lagoon), where they spent the night.

But there is not the slightest hint in this normal round of daily flying behavior associated with tidal rhythms and nocturnal rest, at least as far as I have been able to tell, that can help us understand the knots' sophisticated formation flying. Perhaps the apparent "single will" that seems to control the phenomenon is merely a vivid extension of their natural proclivity for gathering in flocks. Of the numerous theories that have been advanced to explain flocking, the two most relevant to shorebird behavior suggest that it either acts as a defense against predators or provides a kind of "information center" where the birds learn which direction to head for the richest feeding sites by watching and following the crowd. The former theory, in certain specific circumstances, seems the more likely explanation: often knots will remain in the same flock for the entire day but constantly change their location within the flock dozens of times.

On the ground, however, the knots use a different strategy to defend themselves, generally taking care to select resting spots that afford a clear view of the surrounding territory. They need to detect raptors early enough not only to get airborne but also to build up to the rapid speeds necessary for evasive aerobatic maneuvers. At Rio Grande do Sul, in Tierra del Fuego, their favorite retreat was a sand spit at a river mouth that provided excellent visibility of both the shoreline and the landward uplands. This strategy, which is followed at virtually all layovers on the annual migratory circuit, is enhanced by the birds' keen sight and hearing.

Once at Lagoa do Peixe, a brackish lagoon and important red-knot stopover in southern Brazil, several of my colleagues and I tried to catch, band, and mark some specimens in the dense flocks resting in a shallow lagoon. Each time we drew near, however, the red knots would notice and abruptly take flight. Finally, on one especially windy and cloudy night, we did manage to get quite close to a flock resting in a tight group about one hundred yards from shore. In the beam of our flashlights, they were for a moment a small, dark island of subtle motion, eerily murmuring their characteristically plaintive calls. But, detected yet again, we were startled by the sight of the "island" rising ten feet off the water and bolting horizontally to a more remote part of the lagoon.

In the same manner, the approach of aerial predators will alarm a flock of resting red knots, triggering an evasive formation flight. Falcons, common along the Argentine coast, appear to be the main threat to wintering or migrating knots there. Consequently, formation flights take up much of the birds' time; an especially frightened flock may stay aloft for a half hour or longer. Their group cohesion is remarkable: the instant the threatening raptor is sighted, the flock tightens and rises in

These red knots take to the air in sudden alarm, as indicated by the lower echelon of birds flying off so low to the water.

flight, gaining altitude as swiftly as possible before the enemy can attack. The flocking response of the knots and other shorebirds has probably developed because the predator, which typically tries to target an individual bird as prey, will become confused by the shimmering, kaleidoscopic maneuvers of a dense, wheeling flock. When the raptor gets near enough to attack, the group descends rapidly, gaining speed as the knots twist and turn in unison.

Near sunset one day in Lagoa do Peixe, a distant yell from my friend Ted alerted me to a peregrine falcon suddenly appearing from the sand dunes bordering the east side of the lagoon. The knots had already spotted the predator, but not quickly enough to set up their aerial defense. Moving as a single organism, they tried to fly up to a position above the falcon, but it was arrowing in at such high speed, as if anticipating their tactic, that it easily swooped above them with a single stroke of its powerful wings.

Folding them toward its body, pumping with short, shallow beats for added speed, it dived incredibly quickly toward the birds, which reacted by plummeting toward the earth, splitting into two or three smaller groups headed in different directions. After what looked like an instant of indecision, the falcon chose one of the groups and raced toward it.

Now completely silent, the knots dived frantically toward the shallow lagoon water, becoming slightly less cohesive as each millisecond passed. It looked as if they were going to crash a few feet in front of me. I thought I saw terror in the eyes of the lead birds. But barely two or three feet above the water, in a series of twists and maneuvers too fast for me to fathom, the flock suddenly tightened up, pulled out of the dive, and headed north, all the while zigging and zagging amazingly in complete unison.

Awestruck by these aerobatics, I was brought back to reality by a sound like ripping fabric. About thirty feet in front of me, a single knot had seemingly fallen from the bottom of the flock as it soared off, and was trying to plunge beneath the surface of the water, which was only an inch or two deep. Coming up behind was the falcon, whose outstretched wings were making the ripping sound as it flew at perhaps eighty miles an hour. Deftly adjusting its trajectory toward the knot, it curved upward just above its prey while dropping its talons, toes held tightly to form a kind of club. The falcon struck quickly somewhere on the topside of the knot, which was now tumbling out of control on the water. Looping high overhead the predator made another pass, was distracted momentarily by a puff of knot feathers downwind, snatched its quarry, and headed off to dine on a fencepost on the west side of the lagoon. A scene that was actually played out in seconds remains in memory a dramatically sustained struggle.

Close relatives of red knots, the dunlins, have been observed taking at least three distinctly different maneuvers to evade an attacking raptor. Gathering in densely packed spherical or elliptical flocks, they alternately flash their dark upper and light lower coloration in unison, evidently baffling the enemy with this flickering display. The dunlins will also create a distracting wave of movement that ripples vertically or horizontally through the entire formation as they fly. Or they will ascend synchronously in a towering vertical column that will display elements of both the flashing and rippling maneuvers. Whatever the technique chosen by a flock of shorebirds, it is the flock's cohesion itself that provides defense. When a single bird becomes isolated from the speeding group, as often happens when a pursued flock suddenly splits as an evasive tactic, it becomes dangerously vulnerable.

Whenever I visit the red knots' wintering grounds along the Patagonian coast, I find myself marveling again at their molting process, which continues even near the time when they must store up nourishment for their return flight to the Arctic. In other words, they must not only refuel for their journey but must also reequip themselves with new flight feathers, the part of their anatomy that is most important to executing their Olympian migratory journey.

Indeed, one cannot readily conceive of a better physical adaptation to serve the purposes of flight, for feathers are both lightweight and structurally sound. Because they are also well suited for the display of colors, they play an essential role in the complex systems of visual communication and protective coloration that characterize the world of birds. Finally, incorporating some specialized modifications, the feather has evolved to become one of the most effective insulators of any natural material, a matter of no small importance to creatures that have unusually high metabolic rates and body temperatures.

To continue functioning at optimum levels, feathers require a considerable amount of maintenance, not unlike the vital components of our flying machines. If the adjacent barbs of a flight feather's vane become separated, for example, its integrity will be disrupted. The shorebird repairs the problem by drawing the feather between the upper and lower parts of its bill, much as a human might use thumb and forefinger, in order to realign the ruffled feathers to their proper positions. In addition, this preening action maintains properties of insulation and minimizes wear caused by abrasion. It also occupies much of a bird's time during the day, since the bill is the only tool available for this essential activity. From informal observations we have made at migration stopover areas, our Manomet team has come to believe that a shorebird may need to spend between two and four hours preening every day, that is, from one to two hours during each high tide.

Feathers are actually alive only during a relatively brief growing period. Once grown, moreover, they are subject to continual wear and abrasion, especially at the tips. For these reasons all feathers have to be shed and replaced in the periodic process known as molting. For wading birds like the red knot, flight feathers are typically renewed once a year and body feathers twice: in autumn, to produce a less conspicuous winter plumage, and in the spring, to create the colorful breeding plumage.

The critically important molting of the red knot's flight feathers occurs during winter foraging for many reasons. First, an abundance of food is essential during molting, since the process requires the birds to expend additional energy; they have to do their commuting, in other words, with a disrupted airfoil. Second, it is obviously more feasible to molt during this relatively sedentary period rather than at other times of the year when the bird must sustain flight. Finally, since feathers are used to prevent heat loss, it is logical that molting occurs during these warm

A mixed flock of birds rises up in orderly ranks. Laughing gulls are on the top, then red knots in the middle, with ruddy turnstones below, recognizable by their white heads, calico back feathers, and distinctive black chests.

months of the austral summer. In sum, everything that we have been able to learn about molting suggests that it is a physiologically taxing activity best undertaken at a time and place where other demands on energy supply are minimal and protein is plentiful.

The necessity of molting may be one of the principal factors in the red knot's migration to the tip of South America. It takes about one hundred days for the knot to replace its primary feathers. According to our field research at Bahia San Sebastian, molting begins in the Tierra del Fuego region by mid-to-late October and is ongoing in the primary, or first five inner, feathers[2] of virtually all of the birds by December. By February, molting has been completed, just in time for the lift-off for migration toward the north.

Heading North through Brazil to Delaware Bay

North Atlantic Ocean

Delaware Bay

NORTH AMERICA

Cape Henlopen, Delaware

Delmarva Peninsula

Cobb's Island, Virginia

Wassaw Island, Georgia

Caribbean Sea

7000 miles

Pacific Ocean

São Luis,
Brazil

SOUTH AMERICA

Porto Alegre, Brazil

Pinhal, Brazil

Lagoa do Peixe

Rio Grande, Brazil

1750 miles

Golfo San José

Peninsula Valdez

Golfo Nuevo

Golfo San Jorge

50

As the days get shorter in Argentina, these red knots forage for bivalves on the kind of gently sloping beach they prefer because it provides so much feeding area at low tide.

CHAPTER TWO

March through April

*I*N MARCH THE COOL, brief summer of southern Patagonia and Tierra del Fuego turns briskly autumnal, signaling the next phase of the red knots' migratory cycle. Most birds will have molted their flight feathers by mid-February; the others will finish by mid-March, when it becomes time to begin the long, arduous journey northward to the arctic breeding grounds.

Besides, the approach of winter makes low-tide feeding increasingly difficult. The knot will need to increase its average weight, which has typically fallen to between 125 and 150 grams, to 200 grams. The cold drastically cuts down the activity levels of intertidal animal prey, while the decreasing length of the day makes it less likely that two low tides will occur during daylight hours, thus shortening the available feeding time. (By contrast, a considerable number of shorebirds do find it possible to winter far to the north in Europe, even at high latitudes in the British Isles, because the warm ocean currents there will typically protect intertidal areas from freezing. An unusually severe winter along the North Sea will, however, cause a sharp increase in shorebird mortality.)

When the red knots lift off from the southernmost stretches of *restinga,* retreating from the austral, or southern, autumn toward boreal, or arctic, spring, they head toward Peninsula Valdez on the central coast of

Argentina. Nearly an island, the peninsula is connected to the mainland of Chubut Province only by a narrow isthmus with Golfo Nuevo to the south and Golfo San José to the north. The shores of these sheltered bays tend to be immense tidal sand flats, abundant with such invertebrate life as thumbnail-sized tellin clams and polychaete worms. The red knots evidently thrive on this rich food source.

When our Manomet team surveyed the area in 1981[3], we estimated that about twenty thousand knots paused to feed there during the season, with numbers peaking during the first ten days or so of April. Almost all pushed on northward by 20 April at the latest.

The tides in this area are truly extraordinary. In one bay, Golfo San Jorge, for example, the tidal flux is on the order of thirty-five to forty feet. Consequently, the same flats where red knots feed at low tide may have southern right whales grazing over them during high tide. Because much of the Golfo San Jorge coast has huge cliffs bordering the upland shore of the flats, we were able to walk along the precipitous verge at high tide and look down on feeding whales and their young. Only a relative few of these engaging mammals remain through March; most leave a month or two earlier.

Before leaving Peninsula Valdez, each knot must engage continuously in the critically important task of acquiring, storing, and expanding a comparatively enormous reserve of fat. Otherwise it would be unable to complete the series of marathon flights that take it from the sub-antarctic to the Arctic. The drastic weight changes the red knot manages during this cycle are unlike anything in human experience, or indeed in the experience of any other mammals.

The knot prepares for a prolonged flight by adding fat for fuel, evidently in direct proportion to the length and duration of the ensuing flight. Migrants that will cover moderate distances on nonstop flights, like the knots we studied at Peninsula Valdez in 1981, generally add less than 30 percent to their weight, while those with longer journeys to complete will lay on considerably more. Knots laying over in southern

On the broad tidal flats at Peninsula Valdez, water collects in gullies between the ridges of the beach. This residual water makes it easier for red knots to work their bills into the sand to feed.

At Lagoa de Peixe, forty-foot-long "mist nets" flare out at sunset, posed to ensnare red knots for tagging. When the birds take off from their roosting site in the shallow waters, researchers let out a sharp yell, causing the knots to descend suddenly into the flexible webbing.

Brazil may increase their weight by as much as 80 percent when preparing to fly to the mid-Atlantic coast of the United States. If necessary a bird with a fat-free weight of 120 grams can gain as much as 130 grams in a month of feeding, more than doubling its weight. In human terms this would be equivalent to a weight increase from 140 to 270 pounds in a month, roughly a rate of four pounds a day! After storing this fuel, the knot might then fly as far as five thousand miles in five-and-one-half days, using up enough fat to cause its weight to drop back to 130 or 140 grams. Even if it does make a stop or two along the way, it does not take time to add or replace a significant amount of fat before reaching the next staging area. Thus, the resources in Brazil are essential to this leg of its annual journey.

In effect the red knot is an amazingly efficient machine for converting marine invertebrates into forward motion through the air. Its rate of caloric consumption during a migratory flight is about one-tenth of a kilocalorie per gram per hour of travel. (One kilocalorie equals the unit of heat required to raise the temperature of one kilogram of water by one degree Celsius.) But even within the same species, the amount of fat added will vary. Knots departing Peninsula Valdez are considerably fatter than when they take off later in the cycle from the New Jersey shore toward their final destination in the Arctic, although plenty of food is available at both.

Knots and other birds do not lay on this fat simply by eating more: to gain and lose fat in such quantity and at such an accelerated pace requires extraordinary adaptive abilities. When not making ready for migration, they generally carry less than 5 percent of their weight as fat. But as the time for migration nears, some factor, quite possibly the alteration in the hours of daylight, triggers various hormonal changes. For example, hormones are secreted that shunt the mechanisms of food digestion away from the normal processing of carbohydrates into the production of fat. Other hormones stimulate a ravenous hunger, although an increase in daily feeding time is not necessarily prerequisite to the red knot's rapid accumulation and storage of fat.

Even when not migrating, shorebirds can accumulate fat quickly. If exceptionally cold weather develops, as may happen in the case of shorebirds that winter in the United Kingdom, fat may be laid on during the weeks when threatening cold weather is most likely to occur, evidently to help ensure survival in the event of spells when food will be hard to find.

In sharp contrast to human capabilities, the evidence suggests that fat birds must fly faster than thin birds, because their maximum-range velocity—and the lift that comes from their wings—varies in proportion to their body weight. A gram of fat contains roughly eight times more energy than a gram of protein; so, for birds at least, fat is a much better "fuel package" to carry in flight. The nonfat substances largely constitute ballast, only a minimum of which is desirable, to reduce the energy costs of flight. Amazingly, some of the nonfat components of the body begin to lose weight as the bird prepares for its journey, while others, such as muscle, increase in weight to power the flight and act as a reserve of protein.

Because these birds can not possibly complete the next leg of their migratory cycle without sufficient food to produce fat, staging areas like Peninsula Valdez are indispensable to the survival of entire flocks. For red knots, as for other shorebirds, these areas, with their rich and dependable sources of provender, are the same year in and year out. What would happen if this veritable army traveling on its stomach lost one of the staging areas to adverse environmental conditions or to human-made or natural interference? Our research gives us good reason to infer disastrous consequences.

The weights of red knots captured just before leaving Peninsula Valdez suggest that they build up reserves of fat large enough to carry them the nine hundred miles nonstop to either of two essential layovers on the northward migration: Lagoa do Peixe, about ninety miles south of the city of Porto Alegre, or a specific stretch of beach in southern Brazil on the Rio Grande do Sul coast. In a research trip to Lagoa do Peixe in April and May 1984, a group of Brazilian students and I captured knots that generally weighed more than birds ever measured anywhere else—strong evidence that the lagoon and environs provide a staging area for an unusually long and demanding flight, perhaps even the several-thousand-mile trip from these Atlantic Ocean beaches to the North Atlantic beaches of the United States.

Flying over the Rio Grande do Sul coast in a light plane at an altitude of roughly 65 to 165 feet, our team discerned two major concentrations of knots: the first on the southern third of the lagoon itself, the second along the ocean shore for eighteen to nineteen miles south from Pinhal, a town some one hundred miles north of the lagoon. We estimated a minimum of eleven thousand knots at the first location, plus ten thousand near Pinhal. Despite the relative proximity of the two sites—that is, for birds that routinely travel hundreds or thousands of miles nonstop—the groups appeared to be separate and distinct. We saw no connecting flight lines between the two and never discovered a bird marked at Lagoa do Peixe among the birds we scanned by telescope near Pinhal. We did, however, see one bird that we had marked two years earlier in New Jersey.

Our total estimate of twenty-one thousand red knots was conservative, not taking into account the turnover of birds during our stay, the number of birds that arrived before or after our survey, or the birds that might well have been feeding somewhere north of the two sites. Since our working estimate of the world's red-knot population is about 150,000, it is fair to assume that 10 to 20 percent of the species gathers at our two survey sites to feed during northward migration. Alas, we still do not know where the remaining 80 percent can be found. In addition, there were thousands of visiting stilts, oystercatchers, Hudsonian godwits, turnstones, small sandpipers, and several species of plover.

We concentrated most of our investigation on the red knots quartering at the lagoon, a rural area of small towns and farms, despite its proximity to a population center of well over a million people. The waters of Lagoa do Peixe, generally less than two inches deep but ten

Knots rise into the air above Golfo San Jorge, tempting the falcons who wait atop the 150-foot-high cliffs in the background. Ostrich-like rheas and guanacos, the smaller relatives of llamas, are also commonly seen in this wild, desolate landscape.

feet deep in spots, are not clearly cut off from other bodies of water on the barrier beach of Rio Grande do Sul. To the northeast the lagoon is connected to a series of smaller lakes that are both deeper and less saline; its southern end is also connected to wetlands. About once a year, human-made channels are dug to join the lagoon with the waters of the Atlantic, because the local residents have learned that the sea connection promotes much higher productivity of shrimp. (We do not know whether the red knot's use of the lagoon is related to this activity.)

Our flights along the coast of Rio Grande do Sul made me wonder what our own Atlantic coasts in the United States might have been like in centuries past. For hundreds of miles, the beaches stretched out unspoiled below us, with huge dune systems to the landward side and only the occasional small settlement or other sign of minimal human activity. Was I looking directly into the past? And what does the future hold for this magnificent expanse of barrier beaches, dunes, and occasional lagoons? Happily, I can answer part of my own question. Just recently the government of Brazil designated Lagoa do Peixe, at least, as a national park.

The red knots at Lagoa do Peixe feed principally on a small snail that is extremely abundant in the south end, where southerly winds often keep the water shallow. When wind direction and speed are favorable, the knots remain on the exposed, algae-covered flats for twenty-four hours a day, foraging in loose flocks during daylight and resting in the shallows at night. On a single day in April, we estimated that eleven thousand knots and five thousand other shorebirds were feeding together on a seventy-five to one hundred-acre section of the lagoon. At the other principal site, the knots fed mostly on small donax clams and, less frequently, on small crustaceans. Apparently the birds choose those sections of beach with classes of smaller donax. Where there were knots, we found an abundance of small donax; where there were no knots, the donax were either large or absent.

Appropriately loaded with fat by early May, the red knots foraging in Lagoa do Peixe and other staging areas along the southern Brazilian coast head northward to their next major stopover and primary feeding area, the marshy shore of Delaware Bay. This remarkable seven-thousand-mile sustained journey remains one of the great mysteries of all shorebird migration; we have very little idea how the red knots manage it.

Our skimpy evidence is tantalizing. On 15 May 1984, for example, we found on the Delaware Bay shore marked red knots that we had watched leaving the Brazilian lagoon only thirteen days before. In the interim, their first likely landfall on the southern U.S. coast would have been reached after nearly five thousand miles. That first leg, assuming a fairly conservative ground speed of forty miles per hour, should have taken about five days.

We assume that there must be at least one intermediate stop during this leg, although some knots might make the entire five-day journey without stopping. In terms of distance, the most efficient course would take the birds directly from Lagoa do Peixe in southern Brazil across the Amazon basin to meet the Caribbean Sea on the coast of Venezuela. Indeed, some knots have been found and marked there by our peers in March and April, then spotted later by us in Delaware Bay. Such an early arrival in Venezuela, however, implies that these particular birds must have flown up from the wintering grounds in southern Argentina without pausing at the staging areas of Rio Grande do Sul.

A possible alternative route from southern Brazil lies up the eastern coast of the country. In early May aerial surveys have turned up thousands of knots on the shore between the town of San Luis and the mouth of the Amazon River, undoubtedly drawn there by an abundance of small coquina clams. To make this stop, however, the knots have to divert from the most direct route that is presumably preferred by the fittest of their migrating fellows.

If South American layovers are a puzzle, so are the subsequent stops in the United States. In some years red knots have been spotted along the southeast coast, particularly in Georgia and South Carolina. One of the

The extremely plump adult red knot on the right is primed for takeoff on the first long leg of the annual northward migratory flight. The young bird in winter plumage, left, is probably less than a year old and will stay in South America until migration season the following year.

most striking accounts of this phenomenon has been written by Judge Herman Coolidge, who happened upon the birds arriving at Wassaw Island, Georgia, late in May 1971, as he and his companions were riding along the beach in a jeep:

> *[We] quickly realized we were seeing the largest flock of knots we had ever seen. Wave after wave of these birds in their cinnamon-colored plumage passed us . . . stopping frequently to feed or rest . . . I am confident we did not exaggerate when we concluded we had seen at least 12,000.*

Older historical accounts describe similarly dramatic numbers of knots arriving on the southeastern barrier beaches. Around the turn of the century, in the last days of legal shorebird hunting in the United States, a Virginia gunner described a May morning on Cobb's Island:

> *During several days previous [to 10 May] redbreasts [knots] had been flying . . here the flight is along the outer beach, at the edge of the surf, the birds stopping to feed on the mud flats exposed by the falling tide. The sun was not up and the water still high as we set the decoys off one of the points along the beach, close to the breaking waves; . . . before we settled the first flock passed by high up . . . Flock after flock, from a few birds to hundreds, passed in the same line, coming into sight over the ocean striking the beach and following the edge—now just low over the surf, now high up—the first light of sunrise giving them a black appearance. The undulating character of the flight was unmistakeable. . . .*

However impressive, these flights may always have been the exception rather than the rule. Throughout the 1980s, shorebird surveyors cooperating with Manomet mounted watch for incoming flocks along the southern seaboard as far north as Virginia; none were ever spotted in the region. Even when some knots were seen to alight on the Atlantic coast, it was never for more than a brief feeding and rest stop. The first appearance of huge numbers of birds that remain in one spot for a significant length of time is in mid-May on the marshy shore of Delaware Bay, especially the area just west of Cape May, New Jersey.

In sum, the strategy used by knots traveling from southern Brazil to Delaware Bay is not at all clear to us yet. Based upon our observations of banded birds at the latter destination, which apparently made the entire journey in less than two weeks and must have spent at least seven to eight days in the air, we can assume that the knots could well have paused along the way for five to six days, perhaps on the north-central coast of Brazil. Because they would not have been able to add one-sixth of their body weight fat in such a brief time, we can confirm our earlier speculative concern that the reserves stored up so diligently in southern Brazil are essential for the seven-thousand-mile trek to Delaware Bay.

Wherever they may have rested along the way, red knots home into the marshes of the bay along various flight paths. Some can be seen working their way northward along the Atlantic shore of the Delmarva Peninsula, then crossing the bay at the narrowing of its mouth between Cape May and Cape Henlopen, Delaware. Quite possibly others approach New Jersey from the open sea, arriving undetected on the bay side of Cape May. In short, we have been unable to discern any single overriding pattern in these various approaches.

Given the nature of shorebirds and the diversity of challenges they face on a migratory journey, this is no surprise. It is well known that shorebirds, as well as many other bird species, prefer to depart on migration flights under specific weather conditions, usually including tail winds or, at least, winds favoring the direction in which the birds are heading. Midflight, however, given the overwater distances they fly, they will encounter a tremendous variety of weather conditions. These changes must be met with a certain degree of flexibility, which may make the difference between a shoreward or open-ocean approach to a stopover area. (New England hunters gunning for shorebirds in autumn preferred to go out during northeast storms, when flocks would

depart from their offshore routes toward land.) Occasionally extremely adverse weather will force birds to land, interrupting their migratory flight. Less severe shifts undoubtedly help explain why the birds seem capricious in their stopover habits along the Atlantic coast. After seven thousand miles of successful navigation and negotiation with the vicissitudes of weather, it probably matters little to a red knot whether the marshes of Delaware Bay are approached from the south or the east.

What does matter is the destination itself and the critically important timing of their arrival: for the flocks of red knots to survive, they must land just as the bay's horseshoe crabs come ashore to begin their spawning season, thus producing another of the hemisphere's great blooms of protein. It is, in fact, a reproductive blowout by one of the earth's most ancient living animals.

The cochina clam, or donax, is a favorite food of the red knot found on beaches from the southeastern United States to Argentina. But the bird eats only the smaller sixes among the variety shown here, preferring spat about one-third to one-half inch in length.

A surge in the tidal surf interrupts red knots foraging along an Atlantic coast beach in Patagonia.

The Shores of Delaware Bay

New York City

Philadephia, PA

Baltimore, MD

Reeds Beach, NJ

Cape May Peninsula

Stone Harbor, NJ

Delaware Bay

Delmarva Peninsula

Chesapeake Bay

North Atlantic Ocean

NORTH AMERICA

Caribbean Sea

Pacific Ocean

7000 miles

SOUTH AMERICA

1750 miles

South Atlantic Ocean

CHAPTER THREE

May through June

*I*N THE EXTREME SOUTHWESTERN areas of New Jersey, where rivers meander and creeks flow through broad marshlands and on into Delaware Bay, shellfishers work the oyster beds in small boats, as they have for generations. But a far more ancient rite of harvest is played out here in late spring, as thousands of northward-advancing red knots descend upon beaches rife with millions of eggs of horseshoe crabs.[4]

The scene is primeval: thousands upon thousands of copulating and egg-laying horseshoe crabs and more thousands upon thousands of ravenous sandpipers and sea gulls, all drawn to beaches much too small to provide the space each animal ordinarily prefers. As the crabs lay their billions of eggs, the birds enjoy a veritable melee of gluttony. Here, only three or four hours by turnpike from the huge metropolitan concentrations of Manhattan, Philadelphia, and Washington, occurs one of the most immense concentrations of shorebirds—red knots, sanderlings, ruddy turnstones, and semipalmated sandpipers—known in North America, among the largest such gatherings in the world.

What attracts them here so predictably? The lure is a remarkable "living fossil" that has never been greatly popular with humans, who have described or dismissed it as "that holdover from a prehistoric age," "horsefoot," "king crab," or, most frequently, "horseshoe crab." The object of bounties, especially despised by shellfishers because of its reputation as a voracious predator of shellfish, *Limulus polyphemus* has been

The annual beach invasion by nesting horseshoe crabs takes place as the waters of Delaware Bay warm in late May. So many crabs jostle together that they inadvertently dig up each other's eggs, causing them to wash out and become suspended in the water. Many eggs will be washed back ashore, becoming provender for knots and other hungry birds.

spitefully killed for decades. It has also been harvested in extraordinary numbers to be chopped and ground as fertilizer, minced in a special way and appropriately rotted as the preferred bait of eelers, or drained of its bluish, copper-based blood, which has biomedical uses.

Not true crustaceans, these primitive arthropods are most closely related to terrestrial spiders. Exemplary survivors, they have endured since the Ordovician period, or longer than almost all other animals alive today. Along a half mile of suitable beach during the peak of their May spawning, a patient, intrepid counter would be able to tally a total of eighty thousand or so of the persevering creatures.

It is tidal pull that dictates the timing of their spawning migration from the floor of the bay up onto the shore, where they appear in such great masses during the new or full moon of late May. Perhaps one million of the crabs, legs scuttling feverishly beneath their helmetlike carapaces, emerge then to mate. The males take the lead, moving into the shallow waters near the nesting beaches just as the tide begins to ebb. When the females follow, about an hour after high tide, the males use specially modified claws to clamber onto the backs of their chosen mates, holding on while the females crawl through the surf and onto land.

At the high-tide line, the females dig shallow holes into which they drop their pearly, grayish green eggs. Behind them in the moonlight, along the six or seven feet of beach closest to the water, the multitudes look something like a glistening-wet cobbled street that stretches out of sight in both directions along the shore. Each female will lay up to eighty thousand tapioca-sized eggs, which are quickly fertilized by the male and covered by both parents with sand. The crabs then return to the bay, to be followed by wave upon wave of their kind during the six weeks of spawning migration.

Thus deposited beneath the sands, horseshoe-crab eggs might seem to be easily accessible only to the most persistent of foraging shorebirds gifted with the most efficient equipment for probing down into the nests. In fact, the sheer volume of the eggs, coupled with limited space for mating, assures a copious buffet at the surface of the beach. Perhaps a half-dozen nests are crammed into each square foot along the narrow high-tide line; the successive waves of mating couples scatter their predecessors' eggs willy-nilly. Before long, billions of "surplus" eggs lie in heaps on the shore.

The chief beneficiaries of this abundance, shorebirds and gulls, congregate by late May on the bay shore. The migrating red knots, dunlins, semipalmated sandpipers, sanderlings, and ruddy turnstones that make up the bulk of the seasonal population—somewhere from five hundred thousand to 1.5 million birds—are impatient to replenish the energy reserves that power their arduous journeys. The knots, which number from fifty to one hundred thousand, tend to predominate on the east shore at Reed's Beach. All of the shorebirds, scouring the beaches in their vast numbers or ascending in feathered clouds as they move from one rich lode to the next, are able to gorge themselves upon windrows of horseshoe-crab eggs left by the regularly receding tides. Moving in counterpoint to the relentless, metronomic advances of the spawning *Limulus*, the scrambling, jostling birds are part of a scene as primeval as the Garden State affords. The entire bay shore appears to be alive.

Indeed, the Delaware Bay is a vital replenishing spot for several types of shorebirds that perform subantarctic-to-subarctic migration, no less so than the South American stopovers with their bounty of mollusks, crustaceans, and worms. And for the red knots, no single feeding spot is more important, because the nutritive yield of the bay is so high. Although a single egg contains an insignificant amount of energy—barely .035 kilojoules of energy, or less than one ten-thousandth of the average knot's daily energy expenditure—they cover the beach in such astronomical profusion that the bird can eat enough in a mere two weeks to double its weight. We can estimate with some confidence, after taking into consideration such variables as efficiency of digestion and the amount of energy lost in converting food to fat, that the knot will consume almost 135,000 eggs during the Delaware Bay stopover. The phenomenal fecundity of horseshoe crabs comes sharply into focus when one considers that the eggs will be eaten by one mil-

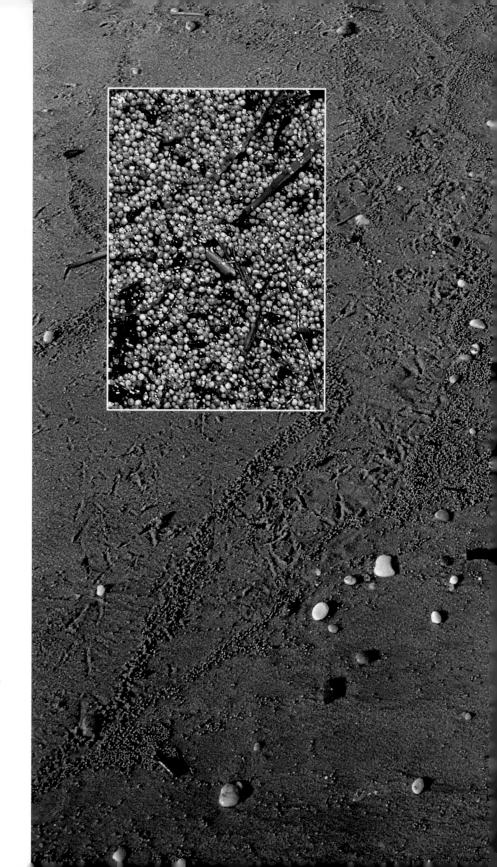

The exposed green windrows of horseshoe crab eggs do not long remain appetizing to red knots on a sunny day. Fussy eaters, the birds reject eggs that have dried out. Only about half of fresh eggs (inset) are actually digested, due to a fairly tough protective covering. The rest simply pass through the bird's digestive tract.

lion birds. If the eggs were allowed to hatch and reach maturity, the crabs could cover 90 percent of the surface of New Jersey.

Despite the wealth and convenience of food resources, however, the red knots do not remain in the immediate vicinity of the egg-laden beaches throughout the day. Usually they forage there only during the daylight hours, then commute eastward across Cape May Peninsula to spend the night roosting in the hummocks that dot the salt marshes of the Atlantic coast near Stone Harbor. To naturalists this behavior is something of a puzzle, because it is not part of an invariable feeding pattern. On the contrary, when the knots stop along the Massachusetts coast during their autumn migration, they feed on the same grounds day and night. Available room is not a factor; at Delaware Bay, just inland from the beaches, there are extensive marshes that seem appropriate for roosting.

One possible explanation can be cautiously ventured. Perhaps food is so abundant along the bay shore that the knots can eat all they can handle during the day and simply have no need to continue foraging at night. In that case they could afford the luxury of flying to the Atlantic side, which may host fewer predators than the bay marshes.

Whatever the actual reason, the morning and evening "commutes" in the bay area have given us splendid opportunities to watch large flocks of red knots in flight. The exact schedule varies with the tides, but the evening flight usually occurs just before sunset. It begins when the knots, which have been feeding during the day in many different areas along the shore, converge upon one specific spot near Reed's Beach. Their numbers, if the beaches are undisturbed, will be immense. If the tide is low, they will forage for eggs in the intertidal zone; if it is high, they rest and preen their feathers. Then, as the afternoon shadows lengthen, groups of tens to hundreds of birds begin to take off and fly toward Stone Harbor. During the one to two hours the entire flock of visiting knots may take to make the trip, it is possible to see thousands upon thousands of them passing overhead.

The unique event at Delaware Bay, then, is critical to the red knots, turnstones, sanderlings, and semipalmated sandpipers that descend in legions upon the immense numbers of horseshoe crabs that come ashore to lay their eggs just when the birds are in need of enormous quantities of lipids and proteins. Alternative resources simply may not be available farther north; the sum of evidence in hand suggests that the Jersey feast is the last possible staging site on the Atlantic coast where the birds can fatten sufficiently for the final leg of the northernward migration. The evidence may not yet conclusively show that loss of the Delaware Bay staging site would inevitably annihilate the continental populations of the knots and other shorebirds, but that scenario is all too plausible.[5]

Because more shorebirds can be seen during spring migration on Delaware Bay than anywhere else in the eastern United States—indeed, almost as many as have ever been seen at any place on earth—this annual spectacle is a vividly memorable experience to the human observer. Coincidentally, the stopover occurs during the brief spell when the birds' breeding plumage is at peak color. We are treated to waves of rich yet subdued coloration and to the captivating dance of surging, incredibly coordinated motion that is unique to flocking shorebirds, whether they are strutting along the sands or flying. The small bits of beach which provide their favorite feeding spots are scattered beside the quaint summer cottages characteristic of the Delaware Bay shore. But when not disturbed by human intruders, shorebirds scurry and squabble along with the resident gulls, making a racket that echoes unforgettably in memory.

As with most wildlife observations, however, the best natural conditions for viewing are both limited and predictable: that is, between 20 May and 31 May, but especially on weekdays close to new- or full-moon tides. The tides affect not only where the shorebirds can feed but also when and where the horseshoe crabs come ashore to lay—a spectacle worth seeing in its own right.

Unfortunately, humankind's influences upon shorebird activity are less predictable. Whether it is the whine of a speeding all-terrain vehicle or the appearance of a nature-loving stroller, the intrusion of television crews seeking dramatic nature footage or the worthy action of scientific researchers, the adverse result is much the same: a disturbance that interrupts the shorebirds during the severely limited time they have for their necessary foraging. Even our fellow bird watchers can be at fault, if they are selfishly determined to get as close as possible to flocks for better viewing or photographs. Shorebirds tolerate disturbance only up to a certain level; then they wing off for more remote, generally inaccessible areas of the bay shore. In short, it gets more difficult every year to assume that the great pleasure of watching the red knots and their fellows will not be interrupted.[6]

As the tide rises, an assortment of birds—red knots, ruddy turnstones, herring gulls, laughing gulls, black-backed gulls— gathers eagerly near the waterline, where horseshoe crabs will soon appear and lay their eggs.

A well-fed red knot at peak coloring rests at high tide, when shorebirds must preen their feathers. Because very few of its breast feathers are light-colored and the russet band over the eyes is extremely pronounced, this bird is probably male.

The Arctic

GREENLAND

Arctic Circle

Breeding Grounds

Northwest Territories

Hudson Bay

CANADA

James Bay

1000 miles

NORTH AMERICA

Lake Ontario

Delaware Bay

Lake Erie

North Atlantic Ocean

Caribbean Sea

Pacific Ocean

SOUTH AMERICA

South Atlantic Ocean

Below a phalanx of gulls, red knots whirr away from the beach in a true "dread," perhaps frightened by the near approach of a raptor or unidentified dark-colored bird overhead. At some beaches, flocks are frequently provoked into such evasive flights by radio-controlled model airplanes.

CHAPTER FOUR

June through August

TOWARD THE END OF MAY or as late as the beginning of June, usually during an incoming afternoon tide as some shift occurs in the prevailing weather pattern, the red knots in Delaware Bay begin to move on. Their numbers have grown throughout May and have probably stabilized around the twenty-first or twenty-fifth of the month. Now they have gorged themselves to the full on horseshoe-crab eggs. By early June all will be launched on the final one-thousand-mile leg of their migration to the arctic breeding grounds.

On a cloudy afternoon on 29 May 1985, a colleague and I chanced upon the most spectacular migration departure I have ever seen. We had been searching the New Jersey shore of the bay for knot flocks, but none could be found in the usual places. Suddenly, near the town of Fortescue to the north, we encountered several thousand knots resting on the beach in the midst of a variety of other shorebirds: ruddy turnstones, semipalmated sandpipers, and sanderlings. Perhaps a total of twenty thousand birds were preening, bathing, or halfheartedly foraging in the sand. The air was electric with the sense that departure was imminent.

At about three o'clock, groups of birds began inexplicably rising in the phenomenon known as "dreads." As if panicked by the sudden appearance of a raptor, a whole flock may take flight simultaneously, skim out over the water in unison, then fly back and forth before settling back to earth. Such flights may end within a minute or two or last as long as six or seven minutes. Typically the birds may break off into small parties in flight, then, upon landing, gradually return to where they had been resting in large flocks. As a new nucleus of resting birds grows, all may fly off again in a second dread, or they may all settle back down again as a flock at rest.

But the dreads we witnessed that afternoon ended differently. With each eruption of flight, some birds peeled off from the main flock and headed away from the beach in a north-northwesterly direction. Moreover, they sorted themselves in a way that I had never before observed in migration flights: each departing flock was a mingling of species. Red knots grouped with semipalmated sandpipers, turnstones with knots, sanderlings with turnstones, and there may well have been other combinations we did not detect. While the dreads in our vicinity were rising around us, other flocks appeared in the sky from other areas, also heading north-northwest, and we tracked their progress with binoculars and a telescope.

Within three hours, as the wind switched to the southwest and the sky began to clear, most of the birds had disappeared toward the Arctic. At most some five thousand semipalmated sandpipers remained on the beach. Combining our estimates of the flocks rising in dreads from the beach and the flocks high overhead, we surmised that we had watched the departure of between forty thousand and fifty thousand shorebirds from Delaware Bay. Perhaps half to two-thirds had been red knots.

These flocks were bound directly to their breeding grounds in the low Canadian Arctic—that is, the mainland tundra of Keewatin District in the Northwest Territories and the islands of the central Canadian archipelago north of Hudson Bay. For most birds the flight is nonstop unless there is bad weather along the way, in which case they will stop briefly along the coasts of James and Hudson bays (or sometimes at Lake Erie or Lake Ontario). But even in benign weather, some individuals stop briefly, perhaps to drink or rest an hour or two before continuing north. In 1983, for example, ornithologist Chris Rimmer saw flocks of transient knots resting on the James Bay coast one day after our Manomet team had seen the first departures from Delaware Bay.

An adult red knot incubates its eggs in the arctic breeding grounds just as early flowers and hordes of insects burst into life. The nest, built with lichen, dead moss, and willow seeds, is on high, dry ground so that parent birds can readily espy any predators, such as foxes and raptors.

Roughly 90 percent of arctic shorebird nests hold a clutch of exactly four eggs, each cryptically marked for protective camouflage. They are shaped to fit closely together, making it easier for the adult to keep them completely covered and warm.

All of the knots will reach their subarctic breeding grounds by the early part of June; some get there as early as the closing days of May. What they find, considering the substantial effort they have expended, is hardly ideal. The problem, contrary to popular belief, is not the terrain itself; indeed, the tundra is a remarkably varied environment that offers a bountiful and accessible harvest of protein, no less so than the staging areas of the migratory journey. But not just yet. More often than not, the knots appear on the scene before the winter snows have melted and before the spring crops of invertebrates, especially spiders and insects and their larvae. Sometimes the birds are forced to become temporary herbivores, dabbing at mosses, seeds, and shoots of grass and sedge exposed amid the ice and snow. The surplus fat acquired in New Jersey is especially important for survival now, the leftover flight fuel becoming a hedge against any prolonged food scarcity on the springtime tundra.

The onset of spring in the Arctic happens very quickly, as is made clear in the account of Joseph Hagar, formerly a trustee of Manomet Observatory. When he arrived for fieldwork in Churchill, Manitoba, on 31 May 1962, he found no shorebirds "except for two pairs of noisy killdeers." Deep snowbanks remained on the tundra, which was still cold and raw, but there were also many bare spots, as well as pools of meltwater on the river ice and collected in depressions ashore. The very next day, as warm winds pulsed in from the south, the snow began melting rapidly; by late forenoon, Hagar spotted a single golden plover about ten miles east of town. By four o'clock the shorebirds began arriving in force:

We heard birds calling overhead, looked up to see them pitching down on steep slant; they circled the slough, calling repeatedly, and within a minute or two dropped into some sunny spot out of the wind, tucked heads into scapulars, and went to sleep, not to move again for as long as we watched. . . .

[The next day, 2 June] Lesser yellowlegs yodeling over the spruce woods in every direction, semipalmated sandpipers well scattered and

already beginning to sing, male American golden plovers chasing each other by twos and threes, short-billed dowitchers and stilt sandpipers coursing over the tundra, semipalmated plovers common, the first whimbrels, and two single Hudsonian godwits . . .

During their first days far north of Churchill, the knots waste no time initiating breeding rituals and selecting nest sites. Some observers report seeing the birds arrive as mated pairs, but it is probable that their haste in courtship and pairing creates this impression. The males immediately establish themselves on territories and begin "advertisement flights" punctuated with their distinctive courtship cry.

The knot begins issuing his three-phase cry, "whip-poo-me," after flying up as high as 150 yards, then gliding downward on the diagonal with his wings held slightly above the horizontal. The call is repeated over and over for as long as five to ten seconds. Next, as the bird slides into a horizontal glide, he begins a new call, a flutelike "poo-me." This sound is repeated continually as he goes into an upward quiver flight, during which his wing tips remain pointed downward. Finally, he launches into a swift downward glide, remaining silent throughout, and completes the courtship display, standing on the ground with outstretched wings held above his back, usually somewhere near his chosen mate.

When this ritual has ended and the pair is ready to copulate, the male knot will utter a series of long, wailing notes, then fly over and land close to the female. If she permits, he moves in behind and mounts his mate, sometimes grasping the back of her neck with his bill, and flapping his wings rapidly until fifteen or twenty seconds before coupling is finished.

With just as much dispatch, the nest is established within a few days. The location can run the gamut of arctic and subarctic tundra environments, from wet, low, well-vegetated terrain to dry slopes and ridges. Still, the knots prefer sites that are at least a half mile inland and offer tussocks or hummocks of grass near tundra pools. During the early 1900s, ornithological pioneer Theodore Pleske found that most knot nests in Siberia are likely to be situated on sunny slopes or hill summits where snow melts earliest. The nests themselves are deep scrapes four to four-and-one-half inches in diameter and two inches deep, lined with willow leaves, lichen, or both, and usually hidden well among stunted willows or rocks. The same nest is not used year after year, but the active nests of some closely related sandpipers have been found with gnarled willows twining through them. Amazingly, ring counts show that some of these trees are *decades* old.

Knots lay their eggs at the approximate rate of one a day. The normal clutch is four eggs or fewer. Interestingly, four eggs have a combined weight of about seventy-five grams, or 60 percent of the female's fat-free weight. It is no exaggeration to liken her accomplishment to a woman's giving birth to a sixty-pound baby within ten days of completing a six-thousand mile hike at altitudes higher than the Himalayas!

During incubation, which takes twenty-one to twenty-three days, the male and female share the incubation duties equally. There is an ever-present risk of nest predation, especially in years when alternative prey populations of lemmings or other arctic mammal and birds are low. When danger threatens an incubating knot, it generally freezes tightly upon the nest, remaining so immobile that an approaching human can nearly step on the adult guarding the nest. Flushed at last, the knot flies off low to the ground in the opposite direction from the intruder, and often stays away for twenty minutes or more. (We do not understand how this tactic protects the eggs, if indeed it does. Theunis Piersma, working with knots in central Siberia, tells of a single fox emptying the contents of ten knot nests. Another researcher Lars Johnsson, tells of an arctic fox that paid no attention to the distraction display of a knot that it scared off its nest with four eggs.)

During the later stages of incubation, however, the male is likely to straggle off the nest in a masterly feigning of injury—half running, half pushing himself along with weak wing thrusts, spreading and dragging its tail feathers along the ground with rump plumage, scapulars and body feathers elevated. He may even drag one wing as if it is broken. It seems obvious that these ruses have developed as a way of luring arctic

foxes away from the nest but, alas, witnesses like Piersma report less successful outcomes. Perhaps the behavior is most successful for luring humans away from nests! Whatever the case, the ploy typically ends with surprise when the bird suddenly takes flight, shrieking cries of alarm.

Eggs that survive will hatch around the first week of July. Almost immediately parents and their newborn chicks abandon the vicinity of their nests and wander long distances across the tundra. The preferred habitats are terrain dotted with tundra pools, the shores of lakes, or the ocean. In its new quarters, the family may find itself in close proximity to other adult and young red knots, as well as other shorebirds, especially ruddy turnstones. Such groupings are a protective device, offering safety in numbers against predators. By the time the chicks are about a week old, there is usually only one adult, the male, looking after them and it seems possible that female knots leave their mates and young at this stage and begin migrating southward for the winter. But even if they do linger for a while longer, they will definitely fly off before the rest of the family.

When most of us think of birds as parents, we picture the laborious investments that robins and other familiar songbirds make in nest building and feeding their young. This picture is not accurate for shorebirds. In fact, their extreme migrations reduce their duties on the breeding grounds, for the arctic migration end point is a zone that will provide an amazing surge of insect and other life for the short summer, a largess of food for animals able to get there. The shorebird chicks can walk, hunt, and feed themselves within a matter of hours after hatching, though they will still need to be brooded by the adults for the first few days of their lives until they are able to maintain their own body temperatures. It is during this period that they are most at risk from sudden storms or cold, wet weather. This freedom from parental obligations, combined with the enormous variability of terrain and unpredictable weather at the arctic breeding grounds, has produced an assortment of shorebird mating and breeding patterns.

All of these different patterns can be divided into two basic categories: conservative and opportunistic. The aim of the former is to ensure

Nestlings gain their footing within an hour or two of hatching and begin feeding themselves by the next day. This infant red knot, probably less than five days old, exhibits the remarkably effective protective coloration that deceives its enemies.

By the time the juvenile knots begin their southward journey, their plumage is characterized by white edging on the back and wing feathers, tiny black bars just above the white area, and a profusion of chevrons on the breast, as well as gray rather than black legs.

that a moderate number of offspring will be produced and will survive each and every year. By contrast, opportunistic strategies run a greater risk of reproductive failure in poor years while offering the advantage of possible "bumper crops" when conditions are more favorable.

The conservative category, which is characteristically monogamous, includes the majority of the arctic breeding shorebirds: stilt sandpipers, dunlins, Hudsonian godwits, western sandpipers, black-bellied plovers, and red knots. Generally speaking, both mates are involved in the incubation and care of the young during the first few days of life. Afterward one of the parents, most often the female, will leave the family in the other's care and prepare to fly south.

As far as we know, none of these species will ever rear more than one brood a year. If the four-egg clutches typical of shorebirds are lost to predators or other causes, they may be replaced, but in smaller numbers.

The birds considered opportunistic have evolved a number of different strategies for parenting. Sanderlings, although they usually appear to be monogamous, produce two clutches in rapid succession. The first is incubated by the male, the second by the female. By means of this strategy, two parents can incubate a total of more than four eggs, increasing the chances for survival of the next generation.

There is some evidence, by no means conclusive, that the sanderlings can practice serial polygyny: that is, after producing a clutch with one male, the female may secure a new mate and lay his eggs—and perhaps even continue the sequence with additional males. This strategy would be advantageous during the years when food is unusually abundant, allowing the mother to replenish rapidly the energy reserves needed for laying so many eggs. On the other hand, there is at least one possible disadvantage to serial polygyny: females have less time to be selective in choosing mates because of the need to lay the clutches in rapid succession.

In the similar strategy of polyandry, the female shorebird also produces a series of clutches with a series of males, but there is an important difference: the males care for the clutches without any help from their mates.

By contrast, the males of some shorebird species practice polygyny, mating simultaneously or in rapid succession with successive females, then flying off and leaving all parental care to the mother. In some sandpiper species—the white-rumped, curlew, and sharp-tailed—the male keeps a territory for his nesting females. Other birds share display sites known as leks. There the males compete for the favors of females that visit to find a mate. Researchers have not determined whether females can be inseminated by more than one male, but the most dominant males potentially could mate with a high proportion of the available females. In any event, males and females evidently go their separate ways after their brief encounters at the lek.

Finally, there are the promiscuous shorebird species, like the pectoral and buff-breasted sandpipers. Females may mate with several males, and/or vice versa, with no pair bonding. This promiscuity quite possibly helps concentrate the energy-intensive activities of courting and mating in or near the most productive habitats while nests are widely dispersed elsewhere, thus reducing the risk of predation. Such concentration of energy might also be a response to arctic conditions, under which time is of the essence.

The baby knots, like other young shorebirds, are highly precocious—sturdy and well equipped when hatched, already covered with down and immediately ready to run about. Because they can quickly begin foraging for themselves, they are less dependent upon their parents than are many other birds, although they may be protected by parental predator-distraction displays. Red-knot chicks also grow rapidly, possibly as a result of the long hours of daylight available for feeding in the arctic summer. Their down will give way rapidly to juvenile feathers, the first step toward growing the plumage they must have to fly and stay warm during the first few months of life.

The reaction of knots to predators varies depending on the age of the young. When less than a few days old, baby knots simply crouch and remain motionless when alerted of predators by parents' calls. Instead of feigning injury, the adults will fly away from the enemy, giving a sharp warning call, then wheel around and dart back, flying close to the ground, passing close to the would-be predator. The male may perform this maneuver alone while the female stands at a distance, or they may take turns in distractive flight. Meanwhile, the downy young stay crouched on the tundra, relying upon their cryptic coloration for camouflage. They will not move until their parents return sounding the triumphant all-clear note, "kjut-kjut."

The "strategy" differs from this as young get larger. For example, young which have well-developed feathers will "make a run for it" when discovered by predators, each one of the brood dashing a different direction from its siblings, erratically shifting directions as it heads for cover.

Evolution could hardly have worked out a swifter schedule for the development of red-knot chicks, which must be ready to wing off on their first migratory flight within weeks of their hatch. Their mothers are gone by mid-July; their fathers disappear about twenty days later. The young must take care of themselves until late August, when they follow their parents to the ancient way stations of the southward migration. To resurrect our analogy to human maternity, it is as if the sixty-pound baby, now merely six weeks old, must stride off and emulate its mother's six-thousand-mile trans-Himalayan trek, in the opposite direction.

Heading South through Canada and the U.S.

Hudson Bay

Cape Henrietta Maria

James Bay

Fort Albany •

•• Moose Factory

Longridge Point

North Point

Bay of Fundy

Scituate
and Plymouth
Beaches

Orleans, MA

Boston, MA •

Chatham, MA

Monomoy Island

Forsythe National
Wildlife Refuge

Great Egg Harbor

Chesapeake Bay

Arctic Circle

600 miles

1000 miles

North Atlantic Ocean

NORTH AMERICA

?

Caribbean Sea

7000 miles

GUYANA

SURINAM

Pacific Ocean

Amazon River

SOUTH AMERICA

BRAZIL

CHILE

URUGUAY

Rio de la Plata

1750 miles

ARGENTINA

98

One of the first stops knots make after leaving the arctic breeding grounds is the James Bay coastline; because of its extremely gradual slope, the merest shift in wind or tide can expose vast areas of mud flats rich with food in July and August. Small semi-palmated sandpipers converge in the foreground as the red knots above them wheel off into the distance.

CHAPTER FIVE

August through October

Meanwhile some of the adult knots that left in July have stopped along the southern shores of Canada's James Bay, the great arm of Hudson Bay that extends southward between the provinces of Quebec and Ontario. Unfortunately for ornithologists, the birds traditionally tarry along remote coasts of the bays, where it is difficult and expensive to mount research expeditions. From low-flying aircraft we can see knots only in a few places but thickly concentrated in each one.

And for good reason. The marshy shores of James Bay provide a resource of incalculable value for migrating shorebirds, offering such protein-rich intertidal dwellers as the *Macoma balthica,* a clam that burrows in sand flats in densities sometimes exceeding seven thousand individuals per square meter. Each autumn tens, and perhaps hundreds, of thousands of shorebirds funnel through the bay from the Canadian and Alaskan Arctic, most choosing to stage at some eight to ten sites between Cape Henrietta Maria at the northwest end and the mouth of the Moose River at the south end. Visiting species include greater and lesser yellowlegs, sanderlings, whimbrels, semipalmated and least sandpipers, marbled and Hudsonian godwits, ruddy turnstones, dunlins, and black-bellied, golden, and semipalmated plovers. In comparison, only a relatively small percentage of the red knots join this feast.

Still, the bay offers important ecological lessons that are undoubtedly relevant to the continued existence of other staging areas for all birds. As Canadian scientists like Pete Martini and Guy Morrison have found, food in the James Bay area varies in density by more than 200 percent from one spot to another. Several factors come into play to produce this extraordinarily large variation. First, marsh vegetation grows more vigorously in areas where the bay's sediments accumulate. The counterclockwise currents that circulate these suspended materials around the bay are affected by rivers and by shoreline configurations. Along the north side of the current, river mouths and promontories offer obstructions, so the sediments are more rapidly deposited there than elsewhere. Second, the degree of water salinity affects the development of winter ice, which in turn has a major influence on the stability of the mud deposits that provide a home for the invertebrate animals that shorebirds eat. Near the river mouths, because the water is less saline, winter ice forms in strong sheets, holding the mud firmly in place.

Because of these factors and others, there are two major foraging zones along the shores of the bay: muddy intertidal flats and saline marshes. The former are the principal habitat for *Macoma* clams. Shorebirds like godwits and knots prefer the medium- and large-sized clams found in the sandier flats on the north side of promontories. Morrison's research shows, not surprisingly, that more than 70 percent of the red knots stopping at James Bay feed in such areas along about 22 percent of the southwest coastline. The smallest *Macoma* clams thrive in the muddiest intertidal flats, where they are also hunted eagerly by flocks of such smaller shorebirds as dunlins and semipalmated sandpipers.

The second major type of zone, the saline marsh, exists in a variety of ecologically distinct forms in the bay. Shorebirds that feed in these areas prefer the zones closest to tidewater because of the profusion of insects, especially adult flies and their mud-dwelling larvae. The former are an important part of the diet of turnstones, lesser yellowlegs, and some small sandpipers; the latter are the major food of semipalmated sandpipers and possibly other small sandpipers. The fishes and crustaceans that are trapped in pools and pans at low tide are favored by species like the greater yellowlegs.

Considering the fecundity and variety of James Bay, why do so few shorebirds stop there in the spring on the journey northward? Even those that do are more likely to feed only in the marsh zones rather than in the muddy or sandy intertidal flats that bustle with activity in the autumn. To date, this question has not been extensively studied, but we can speculate that birds pausing in early spring probably find a greatly diminished invertebrate population. The essential sediments have been churned up and shifted by winter ice and the breakup of spring thaw. The ice has only recently receded from the shoreline. The invertebrates will not replenish their numbers until they have passed through the spring and summer reproduction periods.

From James Bay the red knots fly about six hundred miles nonstop overland and virtually overnight, alighting the morning after they leave at points as distant from each other as the Canadian Maritime Provinces or the beaches of the Virginia coast. The most important of the landing sites, however, lie along the New England and Middle Atlantic coasts between Cape Cod and Chesapeake bays, particularly in Massachusetts.

Adult knots begin arriving at these stopovers between late July and early August, but in an order that perplexes us still. Have the birds in this vanguard departed unusually early from the breeding grounds, perhaps because they have been unable to breed? Or are they primarily females, proof that the female red knot does indeed tend to leave the tundra very soon after her eggs are hatched?

Size is the only practical way of distinguishing between the sexes at this season: females are only slightly larger. But to date, unfortunately, measurements of knots caught on the Massachusetts coast have revealed no appreciable difference in the sizes of early and late arrivals. There is no doubt about the timing of the juveniles in transit, however. Having tarried in the breeding grounds, the first turn up along the U.S. Atlantic coast in mid- to late August. Rarely in evidence before 20 August, they are most commonly seen in September.

In the Massachusetts area, the adult knots seen in July and August gather primarily at beaches south of Boston, Third Cliff Beach in Scituate, Plymouth Beach, and two sites near the elbow of Cape Cod (Nauset

At high tide in late summer, a flock of southward migrating red knots flies in to rest at Third Cliff in Scituate, Massachusetts, after an intensive feeding session. This traditional staging area is uncomfortably near houses and the mouth of a heavily-used river recreation area.

It takes a well-trained eye to differentiate the female red knot on the right from the males facing forward in the foreground and standing upright on the left. Differences in size and plumage are very subtle, including the female's slightly duller brick-red eye band and slightly greater number of white and barred red breast feathers.

Beach in Orleans on the ocean side to the north, and Monomoy Island off Chatham to the south). Of the fifteen or so best sites in the state, only these four, plus the Plum Island beaches near Newburyport, are frequented by more than one hundred knots at a time during peak autumn migration. In other words, the localization of knot stopovers is extreme in this area. Often up to 90 percent of the migrating adult red knots can be found feeding at only one or two locations.[7] For some reason, the juveniles of the species do not concentrate so intensively.

Like all of the other staging areas on the red knot's migratory circuit through the northern and southern hemispheres, its favorite Massachusetts beaches are teeming with protein blooms when the flocks begin to arrive. As in South America, mussel spat is the most abundant food, harvested (in the absence of *restinga*) from the scarce sodbanks that punctuate the beaches.

These sodbanks are ledges of old salt-marsh peat that lay buried for decades or even centuries under the shifting sands of barrier systems. They have been uncovered by erosion, usually beside recently created or newly expanded inlets. Although these sodbank habitats are not common, red knots have come to depend upon them for much the same reasons *restinga* makes such good feeding terrain. Sodbanks are in fact the knots' fast-food outlets of the North Atlantic shore, providing a good surface for mussel spat to fix itself to and grow upon, while the peat is just soft enough so that the birds can rapidly jab in and retrieve their prey. Statistics we gathered at Third Cliff Beach succinctly illustrate why the knots prefer the sodbanks: on average the birds were able to devour six or seven spat a minute, as compared to only three spat a minute when foraging among the rocks nearby. After the six-hundred-mile-trip leg from James Bay, that difference means a lot, speeding the consumption of an incredible volume of spat during the Massachusetts stopovers. With our detailed counts of pecks, swallows, and passing minutes, along with our tide charts, we were able to estimate that some two thousand birds concentrating on a single acre of sodbank in July and August were able to devour twenty to thirty million spat in just two weeks.

Mussels are not the only food snatched up during these late-summer feeding frenzies. Next in frequency are bottom-dwelling and surface crustaceans, particularly the amphipods or beach fleas of the genus *Haustorius.* Unfortunately, knots must plow and probe for the fleas rather than peck them up like mussels, so the yield is comparatively little over the same foraging time. For nutritional efficiency, then, the knot remains faithful over the years to those stopover areas where mussels will be most plentiful. We have learned that the number of mussels at Massachusetts beaches can fluctuate significantly from one year to the next; when that happens, the number of visiting knots may also fluctuate in direct proportion. For example, Plymouth Beach was low on both mussels and knots in 1979, but the numbers of both eater and eaten rose sharply the following year.

All the wolfing down of mussel spat and other invertebrates rapidly replaces the fat used up in the red knot's nonstop flight from Canada, and then some. During approximately twenty days of intensive eating, the weight of the average bird will increase from 130 to 185 grams, a gain of about 42 percent. To return yet again to our analogy to humans, this is equivalent to a 150-pound adult's putting on 60 pounds.[8]

Massachusetts hosts up to ten thousand knots at a time; these are the most important U.S. stopover sites during the autumn migration. Another three to five thousand use the Atlantic beaches of New Jersey, especially the Forsythe National Wildlife Refuge just north of Atlantic City and Great Egg Harbor inlet just south of that town. The peak migration periods in the two states coincide each year; Jersey hosts fewer birds than Massachusetts at peak, but slightly more than Massachusetts during the late stage of migration.

We have to remember that the resting places at stopover sites are in short supply and must meet certain requirements. They are typically close to the feeding areas that shorebirds use during low tides. During high tide there must be sites nearby where the birds can rest and engage in such maintenance activities as preening. In addition, preferred resting sites

almost invariably afford good visibility of surrounding terrain, apparently so that advancing predators can be detected early.

Although it has not yet been scientifically documented, growing evidence suggests that this combination of characteristics—a tidal setting near good feeding grounds next to open areas with good visibility—may determine whether a particular coastal location can function as a suitable migration-staging site. When we add the likelihood that shorebirds will be spread over large expanses of tidal flats at low tide and then have to scramble together in a relatively small patch of open space above the high-tide line, it is easy to see how critically important a specific small section of beach near a tidal bay can become.

Unfortunately for the red knot and other migrating shorebirds, they must pause to engorge themselves during the Northern Hemisphere's summer outdoor-recreation season. And their preferred sites are often equally seductive to humans who want to swim or disport themselves by the sea. In a site the Manomet staff has been censusing weekly during migration for eighteen years, we have learned that human use of a barrier beach has apparently caused local long-term decline in the population of shorebirds. Our researchers recommend such simple remedial actions as closing limited sections of the beach that are the least popular with humans but still suitable for the birds to use. Whatever the solution there and elsewhere, management of human use is becoming increasingly necessary.

It is not just their weight increase in July and August that suggests that most red knots fly from their New England and mid-Atlantic stopovers directly overwater to South America. (We estimate that such a flight would take sixty to eighty hours, depending upon wind conditions.) Other evidence is more conclusive.[9]

First, the dwindling in the number of knots in New England and New Jersey during August is not followed by an immediate buildup anywhere else along the southeast or Gulf coasts. Evidently the birds do not need to make an intermediate layover in the area. Second, and even more convincing, a score of knots banded in Massachusetts have been

In July and August, the mussel spat are just the right tiny size on the Cape Cod banks, the major northeastern United States refueling stop for southward migrants. Red knots find it easier to pull the spat off of sod banks than rocks, gulping down an average of five to ten mussels a minute.

Near Sarasota, a group of knots that winter in west Florida includes a couple of birds recently marked with yellow picric acid. Researchers who track these dyed specimens use algebraic formulations to estimate the total population of this unusual band at between five and ten thousand birds.

captured and recorded in South America shortly afterward. A bird banded in Massachusetts on 13 August was found on the Guyana coast just sixteen days later; three turned up in Suriname only twenty-three days after being banded in James Bay.

There are some interesting exceptions to the rule. Some knots—perhaps one to two thousand—winter on the South Atlantic U.S. coast; a tiny number may spend the season even farther north. Apparently these small groups consist of a few adults with a larger number of juveniles—the former, for unknown reasons, traveling along the coast with the young birds that did not make it to the Atlantic from James Bay until the end of August or September. At that late date, the group, it seems, continues south along the coast rather than attempting the overwater flight to South America.

A different small group of knots arrives on the Texas and Florida shores of the Gulf of Mexico between late September and early November. Our counts from low-flying aircraft and our banding ratios show that about ten thousand knots are involved. We do not know where they originate. A few of them, according to their banding, have visited New England during July and August. In addition, the ranks of the Florida contingent appear to swell with the arrival of knots that have spent part of autumn on the Atlantic side of the state. Eventually, both groups of Gulf Coast knots disappear to points unknown—the Texas birds after November, the Florida group after February.

Meanwhile the great majority of the migrating red knots will reach the northern shores of South America by flying high above the open sea for three or four days during late August or early September. The stamina they need to accomplish this extraordinary flight and the navigational abilities that assure they land in the desired location are among the wonders of animal physiology.

As is true for all other birds, the flying skills of shorebirds are substantially influenced by the shape of their wings. In turn the wings have been shaped by evolution to suit the bird's specific flight needs most efficiently.

For shorebirds the essential requirement in flying is speed, not superior maneuverability. They have to commute daily between feeding and resting areas, evade predators, migrate, and execute the swooping aerial displays of the mating ritual. Even so, they rarely spend more than 5 to 10 percent of a twenty-four-hour day in the air, except during mating and migration. Instead of flying, of course, they walk during their foraging. Consequently, a shorebird has little use for the short, broad wing of a goshawk, for instance, which needs maneuverability for seizing prey that seeks to escape among the trunks and thickets of forests. Nor could a shorebird use the long, broad wings of red-shouldered hawks, which soar above the landscape suspended in warm-air thermals as they search for lunch. Albatross have long, narrow wings, but these seabirds ideally travel with the aid of strong prevailing winds, using "dynamic soaring" to cover long distances with hardly any flapping. The comparatively long inner section of wing between body and wing joint gives them substantial lift. The wings of these three types of birds differ in the ways in which they create lift; the birds' skeletal and muscular structures differ as well, either encouraging or discouraging rapid flapping for achieving speed.

For shorebirds like the red knots, the evolutionary recipe has created a narrow wing proportionally shorter in relation to body size than an albatross wing. Moreover, its outer section beyond the joint of the wing is longer than the inner section between the joint and the body. Such greater length at the outer end creates stronger flapping power for forward propulsion but with low drag—thus compensating for a sacrifice of the lift associated with a longer inner section like the albatross's. In sum, the red knot's wings answer two essential requirements for optimizing survival, giving the knot the strength and swiftness both to elude winged predators and to accomplish the marathon flights of its annual migrations.

During these journeys shorebirds cruise at astonishing altitudes; radar operators have spotted them above fifteen thousand feet. Most species typically fly between forty and fifty miles per hour, or at the faster end of the flying-bird speed spectrum. These high flight speeds

The red knot's wing is relatively long and narrow in comparison with the wings of most other birds. The outer part (beyond the angle in the wing) is also quite long in relation to the inner part, giving the knot rapid flying speed rather than a high degree of maneuverability in the air.

Red knots that we have marked in Massachusetts have frequently been sighted in their South American wintering grounds. "Estoy exuberante!" wrote one excited volunteer after re-encountering her first yellow-dyed bird in Patagonia.

are necessary for more than one reason. First, the section of shorebird wing specialized for creating lift is relatively small; higher speeds compensate by providing more lift. Perhaps more important, however, is the factor of the bird's stored fat. We know that a prolonged feast of mussel spat or horseshoe-crab eggs can increase weight by as much as 90 to 100 percent. This extra fat exerts a strong negative influence on flight ability by causing a profound increase in wing loading, the ratio of weight to wing area. Higher speeds are thus necessary to keep the fattened bird aloft.

Aside from the few red knots that we have seen tarrying along the U.S. South Atlantic and Gulf coasts, by far the majority reach their first autumn landfall on the northeastern shoulder of South America—specifically Guyana, Surinam (formerly called Dutch Guiana in North America), and French Guiana. Especially in Surinam, thanks in large part to this tiny but progressive country's foresight in preserving its coastal ecosystems, shorebirds descend in multitudes, more than in any other part of the continent. Indeed, in a survey of shorebirds along the more than twenty-eight thousand kilometers of the entire South American coastline, Guy Morrison and Ken Ross of the Canadian Wildlife Service discovered that more than half of their total count came from the approximately 350 kilometers of the Surinam coast. For red knots and white-rumped sandpipers in particular, the country is a strategic landfall on the route from Canada and the United States to southern South America. But the Surinam reserves may host more than three million shorebirds in all during the boreal winter, including the bulk of the world's population of semipalmated sandpipers, semipalmated plovers, willets, short-billed dowitchers, and the greater and lesser yellowlegs. Morrison and Ross, surveying this coast in a low-flying plane, were able to count 1.5 million in residence at a time. As part of our own aerial survey during autumn migration, Manomet Director Linda Leddy and I estimated a total of a half million, but the flocks were sometimes so large and the numbers so great that our count from a speeding aircraft was necessarily as much guesswork as reliable enumeration. There was a frustrating obstacle: on the one hand, we discovered we could get our most accurate numerical estimates from alti-

tudes as high as three hundred feet, but we could not easily distinguish between species unless we dropped down as low as seventy-five to one hundred feet.

The birds have chosen well. No one has as yet undertaken an ecosystem study to determine exactly why so many of them winter here, but it is clear that an unusual combination of conditions gives rise to a tremendous abundance of food. Positioned along the two-thousand-mile Guiana coast that lies between the mouths of the Orinoco and Amazon rivers, Surinam boasts vast tidal mud flats, some extending outward more than a kilometer from the shoreward vegetation. The sediments there are fine-grained fragments of soil and vegetable matter, most originating from the upper reaches of the Amazon River basin and then moving slowly over a period of years toward the Atlantic before being swept north and west along the seacoast by the Guiana current. The mud of the flats teems with invertebrate animals, especially the small shrimplike crustaceans called tanaidae that occur as thickly as six thousand per square meter of surface. Because the slope of the coastline is very gradual, the six- to seven-foot tides regularly expose enormous expanses of the flats. Finally, there is the crucially important role played by the extensive mangrove forests along the coast, possibly some of the world's most productive. These mangroves, acting like salt marshes in the Northern Hemisphere, provide the base of a plentiful and healthily functioning food chain.

The extraordinary Surinam mud is more like pea soup, generally impossible to walk on and deeper than I for one have ever dared try to ascertain. Once I saw a small boat actually sail through this so-called "sling mud." Not surprisingly most of the shorebirds common to the area have partly webbed feet that keep them from sinking into the semi-liquid terrain—the aforementioned semipalmated sandpiper, semipalmated plover, willet, and short-billed dowitcher. The greater and lesser yellowlegs have the additional advantage of exceptionally long legs. By the same token, the shorter-legged shorebirds that lack partly webbed toes (including knots) are less common. When found in Surinam, they avoid the sling mud and frequent coastal lagoons, the rare sandy beaches, or, most often, the harder mudbanks scattered sparsely along the coast.

On the tidal flats, according to the findings of researchers from the Netherlands, the shorebirds' favorite crustaceans are most abundant closest to the high-tide line. It seems that these crustaceans are feeding there just as they in turn will be fed upon. The Dutch researchers noticed that when the tidal waters recede, the flats change in color from gray to brownish green, an indication that tiny diatoms grow rapidly on the substrate during low tide. When the tide rises again, the nutritious plant-like diatoms are swept toward the shore, probably providing a largess of food for the crustaceans along the high-tide line.

Fortunately, the government of Surinam has instituted a model program for protecting this rich environment. It nominated three large sections of the coast, a total of more than 238,000 acres, for inclusion in the Western Hemisphere Shorebird Reserve Network; the sites have been accepted as having hemispheric importance (see Chapter 6).

The red knots are difficult to track once they reach the shores of Surinam and Guyana, but surveys of the coast taken during August and September suggest that they probably continue flying south and east along the Atlantic coast. In any case, there are few left in Surinam after October. We suspect that by then the knots have headed for a staging area or areas somewhere farther to the east, perhaps in the region east of the Amazon Delta.

We know even less about the next and final leg of the autumnal journey. From the Amazon the knots apparently fly some twenty-five hundred miles due south above forest as trackless and inhospitable to them as the ocean, eventually to return to the Atlantic somewhere south of the Rio de la Plata estuary that separates Uruguay and Argentina. For most of the knots, this flight occurs during early October, or roughly a month after the majority of the migrants seem to disappear from Surinam.

Predictable as it is, the arrival of the knots on a remote Argentine coastline can be exhilarating, particularly to any of our North American students who happen upon a newly arrived knot banded a few months

earlier on a crowded New England beach. Early one October one such student, Laura Payne, wrote us about having had just that experience:

> *I have fantastic news. I did see 10 red knots yesterday and one of them had a suspicious looking yellow rump. You can just imagine my surprise. I started jumping around the beach because of a 'correlimos' with yellow dye. . . . [A]ny onlooker would have been quite shocked. . . . [I]t was a red knot and it had a yellow rump and undertail coverts. . . .*
> Estoy exuberante!

So ends the yearly cycle for Payne's knot and for all of the others that have survived the journey. More precisely put, Patagonia and the Canadian archipelago are the antipodes of the cycle, but neither is truly end or beginning. In both locations summer briefly holds a tenuous grasp within the looming shadow of near-perpetual winter, but the knots never experience real winter at any latitude. They always stay just one flight ahead of the nether parts of the calendar, alighting only when and where the larder is full, living out their lives in perpetual spring and summer.

Perhaps by the position of the sun and the stars, perhaps by sensing magnetic forces or by using the angles of polarized light, red knots and other shorebirds unerringly navigate thousands of miles over land and unmarked ocean.

The Migratory
Chain

CHAPTER SIX

Into Our Future

THE EXTINCTION OF SPECIES on earth is nothing new. Long before humans evolved, according to geological records, massive destruction of plants and animals occurred over and again in episodes distantly separated in time and place.

But today's situation is unprecedented: species destruction is intense, concentrated in time and occurring on a global scale. Moreover, the accelerating force is human interference. As our numbers increase, perhaps doubling within the next sixty years, the eventual impact of that interference upon the earth's remaining natural ecosystems may not be precisely predictable, but it is unlikely to be beneficial.

The south central coast of Alaska is for the most part forbiddingly rocky and fjordlike. An exception is the nearly two hundred square miles of intertidal mud flats formed by the deltas of the Copper and Bering rivers in the eastern area of Prince William Sound. The flats form a vast and demonstrably essential migration-staging area for shorebirds that nest to the north.

As many as one hundred thousand western red knots stop there in the spring, quite possibly en route between wintering areas in Australia and breeding sites that extend from the eastern Siberian arctic tundra to the coastal tundra of northern Canada. Other visitors include most of the world's North American western sandpipers, most of the Pacific race of dunlin, and extraordinary numbers of long- and short-billed

Gradually, management plans to protect critically important staging sites, like this one at Plymouth Beach in Massachusetts, are being set up along shorebird migratory routes. Vehicles are now barred from a small area of this beach used by the birds for resting during high tide.

dowitchers, surfbirds, turnstones, phalaropes, and golden plovers (including a substantial percentage of those that winter in the Pacific). During May densities of up to 250,000 shorebirds per square mile of tidal flat have been recorded. These counts and other information have led to estimates as high as twenty million foragers during the spring stopover. Shorebird totals of this magnitude are unknown anywhere else.

Sadly, as the world learned on 24 March 1989, the delta system and the Sound are highly vulnerable to a catastrophic shipping accident. When the *Exxon Valdez* ran aground that fateful morning, ten million gallons of crude oil spilled out into the waters and onto the beaches, devastating the majestic coast of much of Prince William Sound. It did not comfort environmentalists that this was precisely the type of disaster they had been predicting since the 1970s, when the Alaska pipeline was under construction.

Not until early May was the true extent of the impact upon migrant birds surveyed and assessed, when four shorebird biologists visited the Sound. Their most significant finding: the consequences could easily have been much worse than they actually were. For one reason, the accident occurred before phalaropes arrived in the Sound; for another, the oil had time to harden sufficiently before the peak period of shorebird migration, therefore posing less of a threat as snare and suffocating body covering. Finally, the trajectory of the discharged oil was such that the major staging areas in the Copper and Bering river deltas, near the town of Cordova, were spared catastrophic contamination.

In a surprising turn of events, the four biologists reaped an unexpected benefit from the disaster. Following the path of massive amounts of oil that had surged ashore on Green Island, they discovered a major shorebird staging area less than ten miles away on the north end of Montague Island. During the brief time they were able to spend at this unanticipated site, known as Rocky Bay, they counted about eighteen thousand surfbirds and twenty-five hundred black turnstones.

Very much like the shorebirds that feed in the spring at Delaware Bay, these birds had gathered where they could find immense numbers of eggs—in this case, herring eggs. Although, according to local fisher-

men, this is unusual for Rocky Bay, enormous numbers of apparently
dead and rotting eggs were floating in tidal pools or lying in windrows
at the water's edge when the biologists visited, but the birds were gobbling only the presumably healthy eggs that were still attached to kelp
and rocks in the intertidal areas. The fishermen also reported that such
large numbers of birds were common in the herring-spawning areas
and that the specific areas might shift from year to year. Fishery managers estimated that about one-quarter of the 1989 spawn in all of Prince
William Sound was deposited at Rocky Bay.

As for the black turnstones and surfbirds feeding there, no one
knows precisely what the world totals for either species might be, but
specialists guess that more than a fifth—and perhaps even half—of each
population was spotted together on Montague Island.

In the end, how devastating to the shorebirds at Rocky Bay was the
Exxon Valdez spill?

Unfortunately, there was no comprehensive study, but prelimi-
nary evidence suggested low mortality, despite the presence of a sheen
in the water and small amounts of oil. Lab studies of levels of toxicity
and sublethal impacts to the shorebirds are continuing; the effect upon
the birds' food resources may not be accurately measurable for years to
come.

In this particular example, luck played a major role. The surfbirds
and turnstones apparently arrived on the island after the spill had occurred; their food supply, though substantially affected, seemed to be
adequate. The biologists were not able to confirm this supposition,
however, by determining whether the birds obtained enough fat to
continue their migrations—in the case of the turnstones, to Alaska's
western coastal plain, and for the surfbirds, to the rocky ridges above
timberline in the mountains of central Alaska and Yukon Territory.

But even if far greater environmental disaster were averted by
pure chance—and not by corporate or governmental precaution—the
lessons of *Exxon Valdez* are all the more compelling. The most important, unfortunately, has been rendered academic by government policy:

enormous tankerloads of crude petroleum continue to be shipped through Alaska's navigationally treacherous and ecologically fragile coastal waters. Clearly, on its face this practice is dangerous to the environment, but the decision to develop Alaskan oil is irreversible.

Perhaps when similar decisions are being considered in other areas in the future, those responsible for the extraction and shipment of oil will remember *Exxon Valdez* and either restrict those activities in vital breeding and staging areas or impose appropriate safeguards. At the very least, the time has come to spare no expense in mandating double hulls for supertankers and to institute far stricter supervision of such vessels as they thread their way through sensitive waterways.

Compared with such highly publicized risks as oil spills, nuclear-power plants, and the atmospheric perils of continuing to burn fossil fuels, hydroelectric development seems relatively benign. It may not be so for the shorebirds and other wildlife that throng to James Bay, the Bay of Fundy, and other pristine areas.

On the eastern side of James Bay, the steep pitch of such primary feeder rivers as La Grande provides a major inducement to development, particularly since northern U.S. utilities firms are eager to purchase surplus Canadian hydroelectricity. The first phase of a multi-billion-dollar project, La Grande Complex, was completed in 1985, nearly doubling the average flow of La Grande by diverting into it the Eastmain and Caniapiscau rivers. The second phase would affect three more rivers, all of which flow into the southern reaches of James Bay.

The potential for negative effects upon shorebird species is sizable. The locations of their various favored foods are influenced by sediments, vegetation, and relative salinity of the water, factors that are all in turn affected by the large volumes of fresh water that traditionally debouch into the bay from the rivers now being developed. Although no comprehensive studies have been undertaken, it is reasonable to assume that the dams of the hydroelectric system will restrict the great flow of fresh water to be expected each spring. In winter peak demands for electric power will result in an unusually large release of fresh water to produce electricity.

These changes will undoubtedly affect the subtle interplay now prevailing between the natural flow of feeder rivers and the saltwater currents of Hudson Bay. When the input of fresh water is thus no longer linked to the ancient cycles of nature, what will happen to the species that have adapted to the specific degrees of salinity now found in the various levels of the bay? Will they move elsewhere or die out? What will be the effect upon the shorebirds that return to familiar areas of the coastal mud and sand looking for their preferred prey?

La Grande Complex might also alter the distribution of the salt marshes, decrease the phytoplankton bloom beneath the sea ice prior to spring breakup, and cut off the supply of nutrients ferried into the bay by its rivers.

These fears pale, however, next to the implications of a project seriously considered by the government of Quebec: as the greatest exercise in macroengineering ever undertaken on the planet, a one-hundred-mile dike would be constructed across the mouth of James Bay, turning it into an enormous freshwater reservoir connected by a "grand canal" to the Saint Lawrence Seaway. The goal of this project, which has been deemed perfectly feasible by engineers, is to capture the runoff of the James Bay basin to the last ounce and use it not only for hydropower in the area but also for diversion to the Canadian West and to arid regions of the United States.

The result for shorebirds would, of course, be catastrophic. Since salinity would be virtually washed away and tides would no longer occur, the estuaries, salt marshes, and intertidal flats would disappear, along with their incredibly rich larders of protein. The migration chains of dozens of species of shorebirds—plus a huge variety of waterfowl, terns, gulls, and landbirds—would be severed.

Only somewhat less daunting are proposals for giant tidal barrages, or dams, in the Bay of Fundy, which hosts some of the largest shorebird concentrations in eastern North America during autumn migration. Because of the extraordinary tides, which can be as extreme as fifty feet, there is an enormous intertidal zone that includes huge systems of the mud flats attractive to shorebirds. But the tides are equally appealing to proponents of hydroelectric development.

The likely effects of the Bay of Fundy proposals would extend as far south as Massachusetts, where tides would change by a half foot, but the immediate consequences would fall upon the semipalmated sandpipers that currently visit the two large arms at the head of the bay, Chignecto Bay and Minas Basin. More than a million of the birds—a sizable part of the entire population—stop there in autumn because of the abundance of a shrimplike amphipod, *Corophium,* that prefers fine, sandy mud flats where it can feed upon plant detritus. The sandpipers are also attracted by the good high-tide resting areas in the region, such as Mary's Point, New Brunswick, where as many as three hundred thousand birds alight at a time. This site and others of similar benefit have been protected during migration seasons in recent years by the efforts of conservation groups like the Canadian Wildlife Service and the Western Hemisphere Shorebird Reserve Network. Such efforts would collapse, however, in the face of hydroelectric development.

The eventual fate of the birds who tarry in Delaware Bay is inexorably linked to the health and vitality of a large coastal estuarine ecosystem that just happens to be one of the most important avenues of marine commerce in the United States.

Quite naturally then, economic as well as recreational and residential pressures fall within any theoretical framework for developing conservation strategies for the area. By the same token, cooperation will be required from a host of conservation, governmental, industrial, citizen, and other concerned organizations.

How has development of conservation planning and efforts proceeded on Delaware Bay? First, the extent of the risk to bird life has had to be assessed. Thanks to ground and aerial surveys of the bay shoreline, we know roughly how many shorebirds depend upon the area during migration seasons and which sections of the bay they favor using. These extensive surveys, conducted by the nongame division of New Jersey Fish and Wildlife in conjunction with the Cape May Bird Observatory of the New Jersey Audubon Society and Delaware's Department of Natural Resources, flesh out the information on population and migratory patterns collated by the International Shorebird Survey.

Second, the signing of the Western Hemisphere Shorebird Proclamation needed to be followed up vigorously on several fronts—and so it has. Thanks to the New Jersey Power and Light Company, funds provided to the state's Natural Lands Trust support the identification of shorebird habitats that have priority for acquisition and preservation. Such nongovernmental groups as the Nature Conservancy and the New Jersey Conservation Foundation continue to acquire critically important areas, either through direct purchase or by obtaining permanent easements. Congressional approval in 1989 of a proposed Cape May National Wildlife Refuge was an especially important step toward protecting some fifteen thousand acres, including key shorebird areas. Acquisition programs have begun, but appropriations from Washington will be required for the successful completion of this project. This all takes a great deal of political will and effort to achieve.

On the Delaware side of the bay, an alliance of public and private agencies known as the Delaware Shorebird Protection Committee has been actively promoting the protection of essential resources. In addition, sections of the coastline are being staked out for preservation by a coalition of conservation, civic, and labor organizations, working together with such private land trusts as the Nature Conservancy and Delaware Wild Lands, Inc. Realistically, however, these land-acquisition efforts will eventually cost millions of dollars; the public's political and monetary support is needed, just as it is for the federal and state programs.

In that vein, education is vital. In Delaware, the work of nongovernmental groups and the state's nongame species coordinator has helped foster public acceptance of conservation measures. In the difficult area of conflict between shorebird and recreational needs, the nongame divisions of both New Jersey and Delaware Fish and Wildlife have been collecting baseline information. Both agencies also sponsor education programs aimed at reducing such major sources of disruption as nature enthusiasts and photographers, all-terrain vehicles, jet skis, and various sports activities. The problem is also being studied by the Delaware Nature Society and the state's Department of Natural Resources and Environmental Control.

Finally, like many other coastal states, Delaware has an active coastal-management program that has been especially effective in bringing

The Delaware Bay's beaches and marshes provide a feeding and resting area for over a million shorebirds on their spring migration from South and Central America.

Along Delaware Bay beaches during April and May, shorebirds gorge themselves on the abundant horseshoe crab eggs. After doubling their arrival weight, they fly another 3,000 miles to the Canadian Arctic to nest.

Everyone can help protect shorebirds now! Disturbance negatively affects shorebirds. Carelessly walking down the beach and letting dogs run freely alarms the birds and causes them to fly unnecessarily. Keep motorized vehicles off the beach.

Informational plaques on the beaches of Delaware Bay explain why shorebird habitat protection is essential. Typically, an informed public becomes an involved public, making the effort to steer clear of prohibited sites.

together organizations with different points of view and agendas in regard to use of the bay area and its marshes and beaches.

You are a black-bellied plover, exhausted after flying without pause for some forty hours, without food, without water, and without sleep. You began your flight near Caracas, Venezuela, and it is now Friday, 13 April, as you finally come in sight of the North American continent where it meets the sea along the mid-Atlantic coast of the United States. You begin to slow the intensive pace of flapping you have sustained for the last half-million wing beats.

Briefly the lights of a ship on the water some two miles below distract you from sighting your apparent landfall a mere fifty miles farther on. But as dawn gradually brightens, you suddenly realize that winds have swept you slightly off course: instead of your intended destination on the south Jersey coast, you are about to land in one of the world's largest metropolitan areas, New York City, where virtually every inch of natural shoreline—mud flat, marsh, beach—has been usurped by humans and their works. Forty hours of flying, and this is what you get?

A monstrous jet climbs into view, racing your way from the end of a runway at Kennedy International Airport. Hard by the point of takeoff, as you see now, is what must be an aberration: a large patch of marsh, a few ponds, and a bay fringed with tidal flats. A welcome sight for sore wings!

Indeed, Jamaica Bay Wildlife Refuge, a sizable piece of land on the border of Brooklyn and Queens on the south shore of Long Island, *is* an aberration. Somehow it has escaped the fate of its immediate surroundings, now a landscape of recently closed foul refuse dumps and towering housing projects.

It is also an aberration when compared with other refuges. Those managed by the U.S. Fish and Wildlife Service, for example, focus on protecting wildlife. By contrast, Jamaica Bay is administered by the National Park Service, whose mission is directed primarily toward people, but which has nonetheless become a remarkable success story of wildlife management in an intensely urban setting.

The refuge is connected to the Atlantic by an inlet that passes between Coney Island and Rockaway Beach. During an average low tide, about 350 acres of intertidal mud flat is exposed, a prime attraction for the wealth of wildlife there today. The bay itself tends to be shallow, generally less than ten feet deep, and dotted with so-called hassocks, islands that are covered with salt-marsh grass and that become submerged during the highest tides. There are also several islands, most of them human made, that are more substantial: e.g., Canarsie Pol, Silver Hole Marsh, Jo Co Marsh, and Rulers Bar Hassock (where a visitor's center is located).

Around the turn of the century, a thriving Jamaica Bay provided a livelihood for more than fifteen hundred oystermen, having survived proposals for the construction of a great seaport there. Still, as New York City grew quickly to three-quarters of a million residents, the bay was threatened by the fringes of urban sprawl. By 1921 the sweet smells of healthy mud flats had given way to the foul odors of contamination and eutrophication, the inevitable consequences of dumping more than fifty million gallons of sewage into the bay every day.

Despite this abuse, however, the amazing resilience of the flats and marshlands was able to preserve so much natural beauty that Robert Moses, the famous New York City parks commissioner, decided in 1951 to work toward setting aside the bay islands as a wildlife refuge. His progress toward this goal was slow but steady. When the Metropolitan Transit Authority proposed to run a new subway line into the general area in the early 1950s, Moses struck a deal for the construction of dikes on Rulers Bar Hassock. Thus were created two freshwater havens for wildlife, ninety-five-acre East Pond and forty-two-acre West Pond. In 1953 the entire 9,155-acre Wildlife Refuge was officially established as part of the New York City Department of Parks; management focused on planting vegetation to attract wildlife and on stabilizing the artificial water system. The water has to be controlled seasonally so as to attract shorebirds and other wildlife; for example, ponds for shorebirds are drained in June so that they will restore themselves by July to the right conditions for migrants returning from the north.

Jamaica Bay was brought into the National Park Service's Gateway National Recreation Area for New York and New Jersey in 1972. Soon afterward a Park Service study discovered that 84 percent of human use of the refuge involved bird watchers and other nature hobbyists. Recognizing that the challenge was to manage a preserve for people who liked wildlife, rather than for wildlife per se, and taking into account suggestions from the public, the Park Service zoned the refuge on the basis of wildlife susceptibility to disturbance. For example, trails on Rulers Bar Hassock were designed to give easiest access to the areas used by those birds and animals which are least likely to be disturbed by the presence of humans. Plantings include species attractive to butterflies and small mammals, as well as to various reptiles and amphibians. The areas used by more timid creatures were left free of trails but made visible to human observers through planned vistas through the foliage. As a result, such easily frightened birds as those that frequent the bay shoreline can be scanned by bird watchers from a distance.

Additional restraints on human use included a deliberate limitation on parking space, an effective deterrent to crowding because most visitors come by car. To minimize potential disturbance to the wildlife even further, such recreational activities as jogging or kite flying are restricted.

My most recent visit to the refuge was with four college students on a sultry September day in 1989. Having missed a connecting flight to Puerto Rico, we had four hours to kill in New York. One quick taxi ride and we were time warped: from the unnerving din and tension of the airport waiting room, we had suddenly been set down beside a meadow of bayberry patches punctuated by fringes of bright yellow clusters of goldenrod. Clouds of monarch butterflies fluttered by, winging southward toward the backdrop of enormous steel gray and blue skyscrapers in Manhattan. Two marsh harriers were coursing the shorelines of West Pond, occasionally flushing small groups of sandpipers. The most abundant of natural settings lay in the shadow of the steaming, huge metropolis: it was a surreal landscape.

Migrating black-bellied plovers, often seen in the company of red knots, are equally stalwart long-distance travelers. They fly nonstop for forty hours from near Caracas, Venezuela, to places like the Jamaica Bay Wildlife Refuge near New York City.

Designated areas on the Argentinian coast are included in the Western Hemisphere Shorebird Reserve Network (WHSRN). They benefit homebodies like the wild coscoroba swans as well as itinerant red knots.

Today about six hundred thousand people visit Jamaica Bay Wildlife Refuge annually. Four out of five are bird watchers, attracted during shorebird-migration season by the large variety of species that travel there because of the several thousand acres of marine intertidal habitats and the variety of freshwater habitats built and maintained by humans. Indeed, the diversity of species exceeds that of most other coastal sites in the northeastern United States. A visit during late July or August may typically yield sightings of fifteen to twenty different types of birds, along with the possibility of a rare "accidental" species more representative of Europe than North America. The numbers and variety are only somewhat lower during spring migration.

The fulfillment of Robert Moses's dream has taught us an important lesson: enlightened, creative management can improve wildlife diversity even at a site that is effectively part of a huge city. Fortunately, other metropolitan areas, most notably San Francisco, are beginning to follow this example.

The responsibility for the kind of change suggested by the foregoing examples lies with societies rather than with individuals crying in the wilderness. Humankind must work together to save the home we share with other beings. But just like the individual who ignores or denies early warnings of illness until the body is damaged or rendered at least partially dysfunctional, our societies often seem unable to plan and act until enormous, irreversible devastation occurs, even including the extinction of a species.

Fortunately, the news is not all bad. In response to the increasingly dire projections, conservation has become a household concern. More and more nonscientists have come to a profound understanding of the nature of the crisis: careful management of our natural resources is essential, because our health as a species depends directly on the health of the planet as a whole. Much is being done today to make a difference. World leaders have met to deal seriously and cooperatively with such critical issues as ozone depletion, acid rain, toxic waste, and reduced biodiversity.

In addition, a new era in the philosophy of resource management and international planning is based upon the recognition that environmental problems are aggravated by the drastic imbalances between resource use and living conditions in different regions of the world. Global cooperation necessarily implies the achievement of rapport between the haves and the have-nots, the industrialized and the developing nations. Conservation, far from being concerned only with keeping animals, plants, and wild areas wild, is also centered upon the needs and aspirations of people. The challenge is to find ways of using the resources available to all living things without misusing or indeed destroying them.

To achieve these ends, all nations, whatever their stage of development, must work together to achieve standards of resource use that do not jeopardize global health, while all individuals, whatever their economic position in society, must learn to live in accord with principles of environmental conservation. We have become, whether we like it or not, citizens of the world, and national security is intrinsically linked to international security. Environmental disasters and their long-term effects are not confined by the borders drawn on maps.

One extraordinary example of effective international cooperation is the Western Hemisphere Shorebird Reserve Network (WHSRN), a program that is working to address conservation and management needs that have become evident as we have learned about shorebirds' amazing migrations. As should be clear in the case study of the red knot, shorebirds are migrating and depending on resources on a hemispheric scale. Protecting isolated resources will do no good if accomplished only on one continent, or at one time of year, while ignoring the rest of the annual chain of travel. Armed with new research, the WHSRN aims to ensure that common—but vulnerable—species remain common; it has been very successful in coordinating the protection of prime shorebird habitat, mostly wetlands—a boon to countless species as well as humans.

Now that the critical importance of key sites is widely appreciated, the network's developing international strategy for protecting shorebirds is to identify critical resting and stopover areas and to encourage

134

*Researchers head home
after hunting for colored leg
bands on knots and other
shorebirds at Monomoy
Wilderness Area off Cape
Cod, Massachusetts. The
author and friends found
two knots marked by
colleagues in Canada
and Brazil.*

their protection. The program has successfully brought together private organizations, government agencies, wildlife groups, biologists, and land-owners throughout the Americas in a collaborative effort to sustain natural resources. Shorebirds serve both physically and symbolically as a link between nations, crossing human boundaries throughout the hemisphere. The program of local-level protection, backed by international cooperation, has become a model for other conservation groups that strive to protect habitats linked by migratory species.

WHSRN's policies are based on decades of scientific information about shorebird populations and habitat use, much of it generated through volunteer programs such as the International Shorebird Surveys operated by Manomet Observatory and the Maritimes Shorebird Survey in Canada. Central to the network's program is the understanding that conservation management of a critical wildlife area is inevitably the responsibility of the people who live nearby, even though, in some cases, the birds may depend upon that area for just a few weeks a year. To help ensure that its perspective remains international in character, the membership of the Wetlands for the Americas board includes organizations from around the world. While this board provides guidance and sets policies and project priorities, the network's staff coordinates local, national, and international groups in their efforts to draw attention to important natural resources and to encourage conservation planning, research, and education.

The backbone of the network, however, is the chain of reserves, the threatened or potentially vulnerable sites that serve as staging areas for approximately thirty million shorebirds. There are four categories of sites: hemispheric sites, which host at least five hundred thousand shorebirds, or 30 percent of a flyway population, every year; international sites, with at least one hundred thousand, or 15 percent of a flyway population; regional sites, with twenty thousand, or at least 5 percent of a flyway population, and endangered species registry sites, which are critically important to the survival of specific endangered species of shorebirds.

What protection is actually provided by the WHSRN reserves?

The answer is complicated. Many of the designated reserves were already legally protected conservation areas before being brought into the program. Other areas have been voluntarily nominated by landowners who have made a commitment to conserving them. In any case, there are no binding treaties; management remains the prerogative of the landowner. Are we deceiving ourselves about the continuing security of these habitats, or is there a sound basis for believing that they will really be preserved?

The truth, unfortunately, is that both legally protected and voluntarily designated natural areas entail risks. "Paper parks," legally protected conservation sites where natural integrity has been eroded by population growth or economic development, exist now in many countries, including notable examples in North America. In other words, legal protection is not a fail-safe approach.

Alternatively, the network approach puts the imperatives of preservation ahead of the formality of designation. Even at the risk of failing to secure legal protection, one of the system's greatest strengths comes from its ability to move quickly to seize opportunities for spotlighting the biological importance of wetlands and then work toward improved management by encouraging local initiatives.

Local networks, a crucial front line in the WHSRN program, are in place in Argentina, Brazil, Peru, Chile, Mexico, Uruguay, and Venezuela. Through local contacts in Argentina, for example, network associates are collecting information essential to planning conservation in Punta Rasa, Mar Chiquita, Llancelo, San Antonio Oeste, and Tierra del Fuego. In Brazil members swiftly and effectively demonstrated the merits of Lagoa do Peixe as a choice for a WHSRN reserve, and investigations have been launched in Recife and Rio Grande do Sul. The spectacular mangroves and mud flats of the Maranhão coast of north-central Brazil have also been recognized for their importance for shorebirds and other wildlife; the area was established as a hemispheric WHSRN reserve in 1993. In Chile research is currently being conducted at La Serena, Valparaiso, and Viña del Mar, where a number of graduate students are focusing on shorebirds. Participants from all three Chilean sites have presented information about shorebirds and their conservation needs before local and national congresses and symposia. In Peru the program works with national organizations to review management practices at a national park that is also a major shorebird habitat, and it is helping to formulate a sustainable-use project for wetlands. In Venezuela potential sites for inclusion in the network are being surveyed by three separate subgroups.

In North America WHSRN achieved such tremendous momentum in its first three years that unique opportunities to benefit wetlands and shorebirds were created throughout the continent. The program focused on identifying, evaluating, and incorporating critical sites and on coordinating research efforts. To date the network has established nineteen reserves in North America—seven hemispheric, eight international, and four regional—and has identified over one hundred potential sites. To promote understanding of the need for shorebird and wetlands conservation, staff and board members have participated in symposia, international conferences, workshops, and media events.

In addition to these efforts, Wetlands for the Americas also offered policy workshops to those who can affect the management of shorebird habitat, including landowners and high-level government and nongovernmental decision makers. In the same vein, biology workshops were given for interested biologists, conservationists, and others who seek technical expertise in identifying, capturing, censusing, and handling shorebirds. The network also sponsors international symposia on wetlands and other conservation issues. When asked, WHSRN will also work with managers of existing reserves to improve the value of the sites to shorebirds and other wetland species. Such collaboration typically includes the development and dissemination of management advice, as well as assistance in planning for expansion and acquisition.

In sum, WHSRN has earned a prominent position in international conservation in the Western Hemisphere in the short time since its inception. Because of its unique approach as a biologically based conservation program, it has been recognized by the U.S., Canadian, and Mexican governments as a key source for reserve-management in-

formation and for scientific advice on wetlands, including their importance as key links in chains of shorebird migration. Clearly, the network's
cooperative structure from throughout the hemisphere is helping shape
conservation policy on a global scale.

For the foreseeable future, WHSRN will continue to work diligently on two fronts: adding new reserves when opportunities arise and
helping managers of existing reserves to design and implement conservation activities. By adding steadily to the world inventory of protected
habitats and by continually bolstering the reserves already in place, the
network is taking the measures most likely to assure the survival of
shorebirds. Its goal has been articulated in light of the story told in this
book: to guarantee that the protein-rich stepping-stones used last year
by the red knot and other migrant birds will still be there next year and
the next and in all the years to come.

Important Issues about Shorebirds

Banding

When John James Audubon wrapped silver thread around the legs of four nesting phoebes in 1803, he probably became the first person to "band" a bird in North America. He had also taken the first step toward discovering philopatry, or site fidelity, in migrant birds. The following spring, two of the banded phoebes reappeared at their natal site, confirming the phenomenon. From that day onward, such nesting studies have continued to play a prominent role in expanding our understanding of site fidelity, but research on migrant pathways and wintering behavior has also contributed greatly.

Indeed, the more we band and later recapture shorebirds, the clearer it becomes that they have not only a strong sense of place but also a powerful, year-round allegiance to their traditional haunts, however distantly separated. Continuing the early work of naturalists who followed Audubon throughout the nineteenth century, we have found many of the most important North American sites in relatively recent years.

One humid night in 1966, when I was working on Laysan, a small coral island in the central Pacific, I was unconsciously retracing a route I had followed the year before to band some sooty terns on the nest. To my astonishment I soon caught four terns whose band numbers were in perfect sequence. Suddenly a golden plover darted from behind a grass clump and raced between my legs. I grabbed it somehow and started to band it, when I saw that it had already been tagged. Incredibly, this band was the fifth number in the sequence of the terns I had just recaptured!

A sequence like this makes a biologist speculate about statistical odds versus the natural order of things. During the year I had been away from the remote island, the sooty terns had presumably traveled tens of thousands of miles to different parts of the Pacific, perhaps to the Philippines, while the plover would definitely have flown off to the north slope of Alaska for its nesting season and then returned to Laysan. Yet, although these two types of birds had traveled great distances to opposite hemispheres of our globe and have little in common, I had just encountered them on the same ten square feet of sand they had shared the preceding year—the sooty tern to nest, the plover to sojourn for the winter. Why here?

We are far from having the answer. We do know, to begin with, that site fidelity is a demonstrable characteristic of almost all shorebirds that have been studied in regard to the phenomenon. The few exceptions are notable, like the pectoral sandpiper: it apparently breeds in different areas of the Arctic from year to year and varies its migration-staging areas as well. On the other hand, site fidelity is not unique to shorebirds. Especially during nesting season, it is found among many other groups, including gulls and terns, as well as landbirds like warblers, sparrows, and thrushes. A number of migrant landbirds also exhibit philopatry in their tropical wintering areas.

Moreover, knowing that site fidelity exists among most shorebirds during their nesting, migration, and wintering seasons has not yet helped us solve the mystery of why it is so widely developed. We can surmise that some reasons are directly related to breeding season, such as maximizing the likelihood of finding a mate or affirming relationships within the social system of the species.

But what about nonbreeding seasons? The likely explanations may have something to do with efficiency of finding food. For example, the shorebirds we have studied at staging areas on the Massachusetts coast probably encounter substantial differences in the invertebrate animal populations available to them from year to year. Although there is little precise information on the subject, we do know that certain commercially important species, especially shellfish, are subject to population fluctuations. In addition, the voracious shorebirds themselves deplete their prey, often by a substantial amount, as we have found in our studies in Massachusetts. Therefore, given these varying conditions, it logically follows that the birds will be unlikely to obtain enough fuel in

The author and a student-trainee check the bands of a tern accidentally caught in a mist net one night in Massachusetts. The bags temporarily hold red knots and other migrating sandpipers being tracked by Manomet Observatory.

time unless they forage with maximum efficiency. To this end, as we have been able to observe, sandpipers at Plymouth Beach repeatedly shift their foraging sites because feeding conditions change with each tide. How does the bird know the best place to be at a particular tide, under a given wind condition, or when the temperature of the mud has changed? These types of information, presumably, have to be learned, even at staging areas where food is usually abundant.

To take another example that we have been able to study in some detail, red knots that feed on the Massachusetts coast can always re-trieve more mussel spat from the soft substrates of sodbanks than from rocks. On the other hand, the sodbank feeding areas are available only at lowest tide, the rocks for about two hours longer during each tide. Consequently, all of the knots necessarily spend a lot of time foraging in the rocky areas, but any bird that does not move down to the lower-elevation sodbanks during low tide will wind up with less food than birds that shift back and forth.

Perhaps, then, it is sensible to conclude that one aspect of site fidelity has to do with this kind of earned survival knowledge. If the individual bird invests in learning how to use a particular site most efficiently—and can remember the experience—it would be more likely to profit from returning rather than veering off to search for food at unfamiliar locations. By the same token, other experiential benefits of site fidelity could include learning how best to elude the local predators and avoid disturbances to the feeding schedule.

As logical as these conjectures may seem, however, they have not been tested. All we can say with full certainty is that specific sites are obviously important to the migrants that return to them year after year—whether to half of a species or less or, in the case of the red knot, to more than 80 percent of an entire continental population.

Diet

Accurate assessment of the diet of shorebirds is no easy chore. Today few of us want to rely upon the traditional method of shooting or trapping birds in order to examine the contents of their stomachs, although it is unfortunately undeniable that past studies of this kind have provided a good deal of the dietary information currently available. Instead the contemporary researcher is likely either to force a live captured bird to regurgitate undigested food by administering an emetic or to examine feces in order to identify parts of prey that have passed undigested through the gut system. Occasionally it is also possible to get information by directly observing birds as they feed. Finally, some studies have taken a census of the prey communities and measured disappearance of the animals as a means of determining what the birds have eaten. This method can yield results that are difficult to interpret, however, if other hunters, such as fish or crabs, are in the area feeding on the same prey species.

We have learned for certain that the invertebrates essential to the red knot's diet are small crustaceans, including small clams and other bivalves, snails, horseshoe crab eggs, small crustaceans including shrimps, amphipods, and copepods, and some marine worms. These marine creatures are categorized as either active or sedentary. The motion of the active invertebrates is an important signal to shorebirds that hunt by sight. Yellowlegs and phalaropes, for instance, race after crustaceans or minnows the instant they spy them swimming in shallow water or after fiddler crabs that unwisely scuttle across the sands nearby. But other birds, most notably a few kinds of sandpipers and most kinds of plovers, prefer the "stand and wait" tactic in hunting, freezing in stillness as they scan for such clues as the movement of water caused by worms rising toward the surface.

Sedentary prey includes small epifaunal animals, such as the oysters and mussels that live on surface areas exposed between tides, and the infaunal or burrowing creatures that live underground—polychaete worms, small clams, and crustaceans. The first type of sedentary prey is eaten mostly by specialists, like oystercatchers and turnstones. It is also consumed by opportunists only secondarily equipped to feed on exposed shellfish; red knots, for example, eat large numbers of mussel spat on intertidal surfaces. On the other hand, only a few of the plovers and other visual foragers, oddly enough, take notice of the readily visible mussels and oysters. Burrowers, the second type of sedentary prey, fall victim most often to those members of the sandpiper family that either are equipped for using tactile clues for probing or are gifted with specialized sense organs in the tips of their bills that make possible chemoreception, a kind of "tasting" for the hidden infaunal quarry. Other species, like woodcocks, which use their extremely long bills to probe for earthworms, are thought to feel the movements of their prey through their bill tips.

The dietary information gained in studies at the staging areas is crucial to understanding the biology of the red knots and other migratory shorebirds, which spend more than ten months of the year away from their breeding grounds. In fact, according to recent studies, it is during these months that they encounter the greatest challenges to their survival and endure their highest mortality rates, in part because of intense competition for limited supplies of food.

At the same time, our present state of knowledge is insufficient enough to fuel a debate among shorebird researchers: are population sizes held in check by competition for food in breeding areas or at other places the birds frequent during the rest of the year? Yet an answer may be emerging. To date, studies that focus on the arctic or subarctic nesting areas generally indicate that shorebirds make use of a variety of hunting methods and habitats during this couple of months. Evidently, food is so abundant and the days so long that they can afford the luxury of using many different tactics. By contrast, research at the wintering grounds and migration-staging areas quite often reveals a dramatic depletion of prey at seasons when the birds visit to forage. In Massachusetts, for example, we have found that at least three of the major shorebird species that use our coastal stopover areas cause a sharp decline in common prey populations during autumn migration.

The message seems to grow clearer to conservationists with each new research study: protection of the key feeding grounds at staging areas and wintering places may be even more vital to the survival of migratory shorebirds than protection of their breeding grounds. Although the prey can and obviously does replenish itself, the balance between shorebirds and their basic food sources is delicate and easily tipped by the destruction or degradation of nonbreeding places.

Market Hunting

Whenever knots and other shorebirds were known to follow predictable routes in dense concentration during the era of market hunting, gunners were able to take advantage of their vulnerability and bring down tens of thousands of birds in a single day.

The rite of carnage known as market hunting, a practice that persisted throughout the nineteenth and into the early twentieth century, was never more memorably described than by John James Audubon:

> *While at New Orleans, on the 16th of March, 1821, I was invited by some French gunners to accompany them to the neighborhood of Lake St. John, to witness the passage of thousands of golden plover which were coming from the northeast and continuing their course.*
>
> *At the first appearance of the birds early in the morning, the gunners had assembled in parties of from 20 to 50 at different places, where they knew from experience that the plovers would feed. There, stationed at equal distance from each other they were sitting on the ground. When a flock approached, every individual whistled an imitation of the plover's call-note, on which the birds descended, whistled, and passing within 40 or 50 yards, ran the gauntlet, as it were. Every gun went off in succession and, with such effect, that I several times saw a flock of a hundred or more reduced to a miserable remnant of five or six individuals. The game was brought up after each volley by the dogs, while their masters were changing their pieces anew. This sport continued all day, and at sunset, when I left one of these lines of gunners, they seemed as intent on killing more as they were when I arrived. A man near the place where I was seated had killed 63 dozen. I calculated the number [of hunters] in the field at 200, and supposing each to have shot 20 dozen, 48,000 golden plovers would have fallen that day. It may well be that this one day of annihilation permanently impaired the species.*

Shorebird populations, or "snipe," in the parlance of the day, were fair and legal game, not only for such recreational hunters but also for the entrepreneurs who served the markets of large American cities. A day's bag was counted not in braces or even dozens but in peck and bushel baskets. Hunters for the Boston market, for example, were known to bring down six barrels of red knots in one night—at roughly sixty dozen birds per barrel. From a single flight over Nantucket in 1863, gunners felled seven thousand to eight thousand Eskimo curlews and golden plovers. There are tales, not at all uncommon, of a single double-barreled discharge into a flock killing one hundred birds or more.

What do these astounding body counts tell us about the size of shorebird populations in Victorian times? Or, more to the point, what do they reveal about the extent to which unregulated market and sport hunting may have decimated species of plover and sandpiper?

Ironically, for those days before widespread scientific observation and seasonal bird counts, our best estimates of shorebird numbers have of necessity been drawn from the matter-of-fact accounts of those responsible for the devastating harvests. Reports from bystanders like Audubon are comparatively rare. When we compare a species total inferred from bag counts with the numbers still remaining when the carnage was halted, then take as a third benchmark the population we are able to count today, the result is usually a lopsided curve: from almost unimaginable abundance, down to near extinction, and then, after a long period, a gradually rising reestablishment to numbers in the middle range. Such regeneration has been possible only because of the abolition of market hunting and the regulation of sport hunting through bag limits, which began a decade after the turn of the century. For some especially threatened species, the ban on hunting has been total, including recreational hunting.

The plight of the golden plover suggests the dimensions of the story. In the spring of 1890, about seventy years after Audubon estimated that he saw forty-eight thousand of them shot by his French hosts in a single day, about seven thousand of the birds were reportedly delivered to two dealers in Boston. Undoubtedly, similar numbers would have been shipped in the same season to the other major markets of New York, Philadelphia, Saint Louis, Chicago, and Detroit, and smaller totals to a host of minor cities. We can reasonably assume, therefore, that golden plovers continued to exist throughout much of the nineteenth century in numbers unparalleled by those we have counted in the world today.

But the withering volleys eventually took their toll. By 1912 E. H. Forbush was warning, in *Game Birds, Wild-Fowl, and Shorebirds,* that the lesser golden plover was "in danger of extinction." As he understood, the plover was especially vulnerable because, like a number of transient species, it tended to migrate over the United States in comparatively narrow pathways, typically passing through predictable "bottlenecks" easily monitored by waiting hunters. But Forbush found that even those shorebird species that traveled over broader fronts had significantly diminished since 1875. Only those species that exhibited the traits of low-density flocking and wariness, he concluded, seemed likely to avoid eventual annihilation if the hunting were allowed to continue.

What is the prognosis today, now that regulations protect shore-bird populations from indiscriminate hunting? Incredibly, given the historical context, the highest single count of golden plovers among the counts compiled at 210 sites during thrice-monthly censuses by the International Shorebird Survey has been two thousand. The *sum* of the highest counts at these same sites in 2,161 censuses taken over an eight-year period was just 6,200. According to *American Birds,* which gathers reports from bird watchers nationwide, the highest spring total from 1978 through 1983 was observed in May 1978, when twenty-five thousand golden plovers were counted in Illinois.

In other words, although these birds have been on the rebound for nearly a century, they are undoubtedly many fewer in number than in the days when they were shipped by the barrel to the tables and milliners of Boston. Audubon's speculation that "one day of annihilation permanently impaired the species" is not that wide of the mark. The comeback of the golden plover, as of other shorebirds, has been slow and incomplete.

In market hunting days, gunners could bring down a score of birds with one blast into flocks like this at Delaware Bay, conveniently located near the major distribution centers of New York, Philadelphia, and Washington, D.C.

These cochina or donax clams retrieved in west Florida (more colorful than those found in Brazil) are typical of the red knot's sedentary prey.

Current Threats to Delaware Bay

While the flamboyant depredations of market hunting may have faded into history forever, the shorebirds pausing to refuel at Delaware Bay today face new threats to their survival that are ultimately no less menacing. In fact, the contemporary dangers are more relentlessly insidious, for they harm the entire estuarine food chain upon which the birds depend.

Some indication of impending disaster is evident in the outworn names of towns along the bay shore: Oysterville and Bivalve were so christened because of the enormous numbers of shellfish that were once harvested annually from the bottom of clear, pristine Delaware Bay. Today the industry continues, but on a much reduced scale; the waters of the bay have become so polluted that fewer shellfish are able to exist there. The area is now less commercially important to fisheries than to the shipping companies that route their freighters and petrochemical tankers there in transit to one of the world's largest industrial complexes, the maritime nexus of Wilmington, Camden, Philadelphia, and Trenton. In fact, the bay is the second-largest petrochemical shipping lane in the United States, after the Houston Ship Channel, an especially important conduit for liquid cargoes headed to and from the petroleum industries of the region. Risks of accidents are ever present, and serious shipping accidents have occurred during the last twenty years.

While numerous preventive measures are now in place, experts admit that the frequency of such mishaps may very well double. Some of the more obvious potential accidents involving tankers include collisions, grounding, or breakup. Pollutants can spill into the bay waters from factories nearby. Human or technical error can cause an environmental disaster, as can structural failure of holding facilities, be they ships, tanks, or pipelines. These are worrisome possibilities, even when we agree that a catastrophe of the magnitude of the 1989 *Exxon Valdez* accident is probably unlikely in the Delaware Bay area.

What can reasonably be said about the likely potential effect upon North American shorebird populations? First, there could be a direct effect upon birds; second, there could be the indirect effect of damage to the horseshoe crabs and/or their eggs. As for the latter, few researchers have yet studied the susceptibility of *Limulus* to marine pollution, but our knowledge of other invertebrates suggests strongly that the effects of oil and other types of pollution might well be devastating and very long lasting.

Certainly, the picture is not entirely bleak, for public acquisition and protection of migratory staging areas is increasingly significant. Even so, considerable risks to their continued viability remain equally significant.

According to national contingency plans prepared as part of the Clean Water Act, any responsibility for dealing with an accident that polluted Delaware Bay, for example, would rest with the polluter. The Federal Government could not intervene unless the company involved refused to admit responsibility or responded inadequately, in the eyes of the Coast Guard or the Environmental Protection Agency (EPA). These two government entities, along with the Fish and Wildlife Agency and the National Oceanic and Atmospheric Agency, have jointly made plans for setting up channels of communication and lines of authority among themselves and also with relevant state and nongovernmental organizations in the event of pollution-causing marine accidents.

But it is difficult to devise specific contingency plans because the nature of these accidents and the conditions under which they might occur are not easily predictable. Consequently, most wildlife plans outline only general strategies for minimizing the impact of petroleum spills, for example, and leave specific responses open for development as disastrous situations evolve. In the case of other chemical pollutants, the planned responses will focus primarily on determining the extent of the environmental damage.

On a grander scale, shorebird migration through Delaware Bay and its estuaries may be threatened by global warming. According to a recent EPA report, warmer temperatures could cause a rise in the earth's seas that would diminish the coastal wetlands of the United States by as much as 40 percent. Temperature change of the arctic communities would increase by an even greater percentage. The effect of such changes on intertidal habitats cannot accurately be predicted at the moment, but almost certainly there would be substantial impact upon the invertebrate animal communities on which shorebirds and many other living things, including humans, depend for sustenance.

For the red knots, global warming would perhaps be most devastating to the precise timing of the ancient rhythms of annual migration. The horseshoe crab's reproductive cycle is intimately linked to the water temperature of the Atlantic Ocean and Delaware Bay in the spring; the insects upon which the young knots feed after they hatch in the Arctic live only briefly in the arctic summer. Global warming would be likely to advance spring in such middle latitudes as the Jersey shore by only a week or two but push the arctic spring ahead by as much as an entire month. The danger to the precise schedule of shorebird migration and reproduction has been outlined by Robert T. Lester and J. P. Myers:

> *Migratory behaviors are vulnerable to global warming because it threatens to alter the very timing of resource availabilities that have driven the evolution of migration itself. . . . Hence, those species which currently ride the crest of spring as it moves northward will find the timing of events along their pathway radically different from what it is now.*

In other words, a Delaware Bay spring that is "out of sync" by two weeks from spring in the Arctic may well sever the close links of resource timing that sustain the migration chain of the red knots and other shorebirds.

Just how vulnerable are the migrating birds to human-made and other environmental changes? Although they traditionally use the same stop-over sites year after year, it would be risky, in evolutionary terms, for any species to be wholly dependent on any one site for completing its migration. Their routes are not, like the ribbons of an interstate high-way, completely inflexible paths. More accurately, they are analogous to major oceanic currents like the Gulf Stream, geographically vague but reasonably consistent pathways that may shift location slightly with changes in climatic patterns.

Given this analogy, the question of Delaware Bay's importance in determining a migratory route is related to other factors, such as the competing benefits of other possible routes or the extent to which the bay area has been chosen over time as a reflection of natural selection—and therefore presumably offers maximal benefits to the migrants. Such analysis assumes that certain migration routes and staging areas will af-ford improved chances for survival. Do they? And if so, how?

Perhaps the answer can be inferred in part by comparing the strik-ing differences between the spring and fall migrations of the red knots and other shorebirds. Hundreds of thousands of sandpipers and plovers rest at the Bay of Fundy in Canada in the autumn; few pause there in the spring. Indeed, with only a few exceptions, like the black-bellied plover, most shorebirds tend not to return to many of their autumn stopping places along the Atlantic coast during the spring migration, aside from Delaware Bay and a few sites immediately to the south.

Not much research has focused on this phenomenon, but it is probably related to the location and abundance of food. In autumn the bays, estuaries, and marshes of eastern Canada and the northeastern United States are typically flush with insects and/or marine inverte-brates that have become numerous during the summer growing season; semipalmated sandpipers and other shorebirds swarm there to fatten up.

The situation changes radically: first, the autumn migrants deplete the food resources, then come the depredations of winter—fish, waterfowl, invertebrate predators, winter ice, and probably other factors yet unknown. By April and May, when the spring shorebird migration passes near, the invertebrate population in the region is at its lowest for the entire year, and the migrants do not stop to feed.

In the same vein, many shorebirds apparently deviate from the most direct course between their wintering and breeding areas in the spring because of a seasonal flush of prey. In the Great Plains, where spring is in full swing by April and May, shorebirds whose feeding habits are flexible enough to enable them to thrive at nonmarine sites during migration will divert inland, where they thrive on an almost unimaginable abundance of wetland and prairie insects.

Other shorebirds, less flexible, and therefore dependent upon marine sites for refueling, must rely on Delaware Bay. At least three species found there in spring—the red knot, turnstone, and sanderling—are almost never found in appreciable numbers at inland sites. (An exception occurs farther west for sanderlings, which are numerous at a few alkaline wetland sites in the Canadian prairies during spring.) They can therefore be considered obligate coastal birds during spring and autumn. In addition, semipalmated sandpipers that nest in the northeastern parts of Canada collect at the bay, although they are able to use inland areas during migration. For these members of the species, however, the route through Delaware Bay is apparently the most direct one. (Other semipalmated sandpipers do stop at inland sites in Kansas and other Great Plains states, but they are heading for central and western parts of the Arctic.)

In theory, even the obligate species need not stop at Delaware Bay to refuel. The leg from there to the next marine feeding site to the north, James Bay, is only about seven hundred miles, or roughly twice the distance from the U.S. Gulf Coast. Normally any shorebird could easily make the longer trip with ease. On the other hand, it is important for the red knots and other species to arrive at nesting areas with a fat reserve as large as possible—partly for insulation against the cold of late-

spring snows, partly to help provide the high energy required in the
early breeding period when food might still be scarce. In sum, the layover at Delaware Bay has less to do with total flying distance than with
nutritional needs. By contrast with James Bay in spring, at Delaware
Bay breeding horseshoe crabs offer a rich food resource to northbound
migrants. Although birds stopping here must travel greater distances
from staging to breeding areas, they will be carrying more fat on arrival
than those coming from James Bay, where their food is scarce in May.

Female and smaller male horseshoe crabs crawl along the muddy flats of Delaware Bay. The effects of pollution on the crabs are poorly known. Researchers worry that an extensive petrochemical accident in nearby shipping channels would drastically reduce crab populations, perhaps breaking a critical food link in the knots' chain of migration.

A handful of oozing beach mud can contain many thousands of tiny bivalve clams and other nutritious invertebrates. Researchers use sieves to identify the types and average quantities of food available to shorebirds in specific areas.

Mud

Mud—whether it be the mire of freshwater marshes or the ooze to be found at most tidal flats—is surely one of the most ignorantly disparaged of earth's resources. "The modern world is blind to the life and beauty of mud," as Peter Steinhart has written in *Audubon:*

> *We think of mud as something unfinished, a lugubrious prospect that goes with heavy skies and deferred purposes, plasma waiting to become land or water. . . . Mud has become a cultural metaphor rather than a part of nature. It has become a symbol of abasement, confusion, and moral disorder.*

Unfortunately, human behavior at the coastal estuaries near our major population centers confirms Steinhart's complaint all too plainly. According to studies that have only recently been initiated in these areas, our fouling of the waters and intertidal flats with raw sewage is taking a severe toll. Although mud flats and marshlands do have an amazing ability to absorb enormous amounts of organic waste, 90 percent of the traditional shellfishing areas in northeastern states like Connecticut are no longer fishable. At issue is not simply the loss of shellfish beds and the livelihood of fishermen; the entire ecosystems that serve the energy needs of many coastal fauna are threatened.

The importance of mud in sustaining these ecosystems is not well understood, even by admiring ecologists. Life develops in our coastal marshes and estuaries by means of complex processes that depend upon a number of biological and chemical connections involving the sun, characteristically high numbers of animals, plentitude of plant growth, and the organisms that promote decay.

But it takes only one visit to a healthy mud flat to convince any careful observer that something important is happening there. When you drop to your knees, lower your face close to the mud surface, and watch quietly, myriad activities become apparent: at low tide little animals scurry about in great profusion just below the surface; at higher tide dozens of tiny shrimplike creatures and fishes swarm into close view. As many as three hundred thousand tiny gem clams have been sifted from a square meter of tidal flat! Thronging near you will be hundreds of harvesters—ducks, gulls, herons, and thousands of shorebirds—perhaps more animal weight per acre than you could find on any field or woodlot at comparable latitudes.

This melee, this exceptionally high productivity in an estuary, is intrinsically related to the acreage of its tidal flats: the muds trap nutrients, and high nutrient levels stimulate plant growth. I like to think of the flats as forming the piston chamber of a massive biological engine. Its raw fuel comes from the sunlight energy that is captured at an extremely high rate by the salt-marsh grasses and the microscopic plants, or estuarine algae, floating in the water. This fuel is converted to usable form in the estuarine refinery. First, broken fragments from the marshland plants—be they grasses, algae, mangrove leaves, or even leaves and organic material imported by rivers from the land upstream—settle to the bottom as detritus and become mixed into the mud. There they are reduced by beneficial bacteria and fungi into a consumable form; that is, into smaller bacteria and fungi that can be eaten by the animals near the base of the estuarine food chain, the so-called detritivores. In turn they become the refined fuel, as it were, that drives the entire biological engine of the estuary with all of its plant and animal species, including shorebirds. In short, the estuaries could not be nearly so powerful an engine without the biological refinery at work in the muddy sediments.

With this analogy in mind, we have a better idea of how to look at tidal flats in closer detail. For example, we can generally expect to find flats where there are good sources of particles, whether sand or clay, that are delivered by relatively fast-moving water to a place where the current slows considerably, allowing sediments to settle out. Most commonly, these conditions occur in bays and estuaries as water from inflowing streams or rivers slows down.

The composition of the tidal flats ranges from relatively large-grained sand to silt and clay particles so minute as to be measured in microns. The coarser grains are characteristically found in areas with greater movement of water; because they provide less surface area for bacteria and other microscopic life to grow on, they generally have a lower biological productivity than the finer-grained sediments. The latter, which form oozy muds in the most sheltered waters, tend to have not only the highest populations of invertebrate animals but also, not surprisingly, the greatest numbers of birds, especially shorebirds.

Navigation

The precise nature of the navigational gifts of the red knot and other shorebirds remains a mystery. Year in and year out, these migrants fly thousands of miles over featureless ocean between continents and arrive somehow at predictable landfalls, but we do not know how.

On the two thousand miles of ocean between eastern Canada and the South American mainland, a seascape devoid of the visual clues we humans would use for finding our way, the consequences of drifting off course a mere ten degrees to the east would be fatal. The knot would undoubtedly miss the land and succumb to exhaustion. Similarly, the shorebirds that fly from Alaska to tiny islands in the Pacific must navigate precisely to survive. If they were to wander just one degree off course, they would miss even the island nearest to Alaska, Kure Atoll in the northwest Hawaiian group, by fifty to sixty miles.

In addition to the obvious fact that the knots and other shorebirds do turn up alive where they must, there is other convincing evidence for their impressive navigational abilities. For example, radar studies have shown that the migrants deftly compensate for wind drift by changing their heading, thus maintaining their required course. There is also circumstantial evidence, gathered from several studies, to indicate that shorebirds use curved great-circle routes, as human aviation navigators have learned to do in the twentieth century. Such routes are not straight magnetic lines but curvilinear paths that form the shortest distance between two points on a globe. If this is true, the birds have to change direction frequently midcourse and call upon extremely precise navigational abilities.

Perhaps, too, birds calibrate their navigational readings. On many occasions I have watched shorebirds make their departures late in the afternoon, whether southward from the Massachusetts coast during autumn migration or northward from Delaware Bay in the spring. In roughly fifty instances, I have observed much the same pattern: never do the flocks fly off immediately on a direct course. Instead, they tend to veer repeatedly to the left and right of their eventual flight-track headings, sometimes by as much as ninety degrees, but always veering back in the general direction of their track. This behavior suggests that the birds set their course using some sort of calibration achieved through these recurrent deviations. Whatever the truth of the matter, the flocks do not realize a direct course even by the time they disappear from telescope visibility—perhaps six or seven minutes of flight time covering four to five miles. In contrast, I have seen very high flocks on direct, unvarying courses. Apparently these tracks were set after take-off in response to a period of navigational "readings" that indicated course adjustments.

Research on species other than shorebirds suggests that animals can navigate by means of several different methods: by the position of the stars at night or the sun during the day, by taking cues from the angles of polarizing light, or by sensing magnetic fields. This last is perhaps the most fascinating and least understood of all the techniques that birds might use for navigation.

Although we tend not to think of magnetic detection as a primary sense in animals, it is in fact important in quite a few species, even among organisms as rudimentary as bacteria. Apparently for birds it is a vital means of orienting themselves, not only during migratory journeys but at other times as well. Based upon the scant information we have, we infer that a bird's innate ability to process magnetic information differs little from what a human can achieve with a compass.

But there is an essential difference in the mechanism used. For most of us, the notion of the earth's magnetism involves magnetic *polarity,* the force that causes the needles of a compass to point toward magnetic north. By our standards the compass may seem to be an old-fashioned instrument; in fact, it is quite modern in terms of the vast reaches of evolutionary or geologic time. The point is that our magnetic compass was invented after the last of the many periodic reversals of the earth's magnetic fields that have taken place throughout the his-

tory of the planet. Were we to experience such a shift today, our compasses would be rendered virtually useless. So, too, would any internal
bird "compass" that operated solely on the principle of magnetic polarity. But birds, successfully migrating for tens of thousands of years, have
evidently been unfazed by the numerous reversals of global polarity during those aeons. How, then, if they really do rely on magnetism for
navigation, have they managed to finesse their way through the constantly changing situation?

The secret may be that birds do not rely on simple polarity. In
other words, their internal direction finders are probably not polar compasses but rather *inclination* compasses. Rather than differentiate between
north and south, such compasses would distinguish between poleward
and equatorward bearings. Since the strength of magnetic forces generally increases from the equatorial regions of the earth toward the poles,
birds could possibly use information about magnetic strength to determine where they are with respect to poles and equator.

Indeed, experiments with a small sample of birds have shown that
they have the ability to detect magnetic forces far lower and also far
greater than any they would encounter in the natural gradient from north
to south. Presumably this means that they would be able to sense any
differences that develop during the course of a migration flight. On the
other hand, the few birds involved in these particular experiments did
not seem able to respond to changes in magnetic levels without a sufficient period of acclimation. This peculiarity would be advantageous in
the event that they pass over or through areas of magnetic irregularity.

Despite all of the information researchers have compiled on how birds
respond to magnetic forces, we can only speculate on how they detect
them. It seems likely that magnetic detection is related to light detection
in the visual system, according to most of the scant evidence we have
been able to accumulate, but if so, the exact mechanism is not understood. Nor do we know anything about the problems that, presumably,
must be associated with using the inclination compass. For example,
how do migrants head away from one pole toward the equator during

the first part of their flight, cross the equator, and then continue onward toward the opposite pole?

Most of what we do know about the red knot's sense of magnetic detection comes from studies of homing pigeons. Clearly the pigeons' ability to orient themselves and navigate is based upon combining what they learn by magnetic detection with their integration (and/or switching) of information gleaned from the visual and other senses. This secondary data includes what can be learned by smell or by analyzing polarized light and the position of the sun. Such methods are as complex as magnetic detection. For example, neither sun position nor time of day alone would enable successful navigation; the two types of information must be combined and integrated. On the basis of some studies, it seems likely that these secondary methods are not innate but learned; both young and older homing pigeons that have been experimentally displaced revert to using magnetic cues to orient themselves. Once the secondary methods are learned, however, they become the procedure of choice. Thereafter the pigeons rely on magnetic information only when all other cues fail. For example, birds may characteristically navigate by the stars by night, but when cloud cover becomes too dense, they may switch to magnetic cues. In other words, in the opinion of most researchers in the field, the combination of navigation systems available to birds creates a remarkably sophisticated backup system roughly analogous to the human pilot or mariner's choice of relying upon compass, loran, or dead reckoning.

But birds, in another analogy with humans, are not infallible navigators. Occasionally we encounter flocks of migrants, even shorebirds, that have become disoriented in various ways, including losing altitude. Usually the explanation is foul weather—probably fog and/or heavy precipitation—in association with bright lights. Less often, according to reported observations, birds have become disoriented because they have entered an area of strong magnetic irregularities.

Indeed, migrant shorebirds passing over just such a region in Sweden inspired an unusually interesting study by Thomas Alerstam, who used a number of visual and radar trackings. In one representative sequence, he observed four curlews:

> [They were] approaching in the late afternoon at about 950 meters in steady formation flight towards the SW. Suddenly, the birds dived and banked, interspersed with some gliding, and the flock formation was broken up. Three individuals gradually resumed formation flight after 10 to 15 seconds, while the fourth remained separated. A minute later there was a new incident of rather violent banking and diving by the birds and the flock formation was again broken up. The three individuals soon reassembled into formation, and the fourth joined them after almost three minutes of descent, causing a total height loss of about 100 meters.

In another incident at the magnetic anomaly, Alerstam watched five different species of shorebirds become disoriented for at least an hour in bad weather—drizzle, poor visibility, and low stratus clouds. In their confusion the birds flew in a circle so low that some of them swooped under road lamps. When visibility improved at the end of the hour, the birds immediately rose upward and disappeared.

Episodes like this suggest that the curlews had switched to magnetic navigation because of the weather and then were confounded by regional irregularity. Significantly, shorebirds observed flying in the area under conditions of poor visibility at night were unable to recover their bearings and became trapped for an hour or until visibility improved. Then, perhaps, they were able to set their course by the emerging stars. In any event, it seems clear that multiple backup systems fail even in nature.

The whole puzzle of navigation is further complicated by the challenges that face the young red knots and other shorebirds. Mere weeks after hatch, some time after their parents have left them on their own, they must travel thousands of miles toward the traditional wintering grounds of their species. They obviously have no prior experience upon which to rely; most have little or no adult accompaniment along the way. Some observers believe that these young birds have not yet developed the navigational abilities of adults because they are more likely to show up at marginal stopover habitats. But that assessment is debatable, and debated, for other specialists do not agree that the juvenile knots are merely straying off course. For one reason, it might well be sensible for the late-traveling young to stop to feed at nontraditional sites because their elders have just recently depleted the resources at traditional spots. For another, their tardiness also makes it more likely that they will encounter the storms and other adverse migratory conditions that occur more frequently at summer's end. In that case, their displacement to unscheduled layover sites is more easily understood.

Quite apart from such speculations and other stimulating theories, however, the basic question remains unanswered: we do not know how the first-time migrant red knots make it to their essential destination in the Southern Hemisphere or why, to approach the same issue from a different point of view, some of them do not.

Migrants in the Midwest: The Cheyenne Bottoms Story

During the weeks when the red knots are feeding so energetically at Delaware Bay, many other shorebird species are making their spring stopovers at protein-rich locations along the inland flyways of North America. One of the most important and fascinating is Cheyenne Bottoms, a forty-one-thousand-acre basin in central Kansas that holds some sixteen thousand acres of wetlands.

There are many different ways in which the coming of spring becomes manifest in the Kansas prairies after the seemingly interminable grip of winter there, but for many people the sight of birds in flight is the most welcome harbinger of returning warmth and new life. Aldo Leopold celebrates the signal import of migrating birds in *A Sand Country Almanac:*

> *One swallow does not make a summer, but one skein of geese, cleaving the murk of a March thaw, is the 'spring'.*

Less well known, perhaps, but equally characteristic of early spring in the region is the first killdeer cry cutting through the last remnants of winter winds. In Kansas it may also be the appearance of the first Baird's sandpipers, small creatures that have traveled hard and fast from still-lush Patagonia to feed on seeps of water at the edges of an icy marsh.

So begins the annual flood of feathered life into the Northern Hemisphere as winter's hold is barely beginning to unlock. Swiftly the skies will speckle with ephemeral flocks racing north in league with the first spring moisture traveling up from the Gulf coastal plain. Soon tens of thousands of sandpipers and plovers will throng the marshes, many arriving from places completely foreign and exotic to the humans who live on this productive midwestern land.

At the same time, other life is stirring. For millions of insects, another seasonal cycle of life begins in the marsh mud. The larvae of chironomid midges, primarily an aquatic family, are incredibly abundant at Cheyenne Bottoms in March, their numbers approaching twenty thousand per square meter of marsh. The young that survive will become the adult midges more familiar to humans and often mistaken for mosquitoes as they dance over the marsh waters in immense swarms from early spring through autumn. The high density of their larvae here is an invaluable source of food for birds so early in spring, when land insect populations are still largely inaccessible. Moreover, since the larval midges nestle in soft mud substrates or in shallow water, they are quite easily caught by soft-billed shorebirds.

Among other desirable invertebrates common at the Bottoms is the copepod, a type of crustacean that peaks in annual population between March and May. It is particularly important to those shorebirds who prefer to forage in water than in mud, like the yellowlegs and Wilson's phalaropes.

The numbers of shorebirds counted at various coastal and inland habitats in the lower forty-eight states by the International Shorebird Survey during spring and autumn migration have confirmed that Cheyenne Bottoms, used by hundreds of thousands of shorebirds in a typical year, is clearly the single most important inland site.

The influx begins gradually in March, when Baird's sandpipers are the single most common species. Around the middle of the month, long-billed dowitchers arrive on the scene. Still more members of both these species pour in during the first third of April, accompanied by flocks of lesser yellowlegs, semipalmated sandpipers, Wilson's phalaropes, and American avocets. Less common species appear in smaller numbers.

But it is during the first third of May that the visiting population of shorebirds swells dramatically, a surge that has averaged more than 140,000 birds a day over thirteen annual censuses. On a single day in May 1982, International Shorebird Survey cooperator Ed Martinez counted an astonishing total of more than 410,000 arrivals. The new visitors always include white-rumped sandpipers and Hudsonian god-wits, along with even more semipalmated sandpipers. A little later, around the middle of the month, tens of thousands of stilt sandpipers, which are hard to find in many areas of the United States, descend to feed on the chironomids. In this enterprise they are joined by pectoral sandpipers and small numbers of various other species.

But these impressive statistics do not really put the fundamental importance of Cheyenne Bottoms to world shorebird populations in revealing perspective. To assess the role played by the Bottoms, we have to infer from relative numbers. For example, counts routinely made each year by the International Shorebird Survey network of observers unequivocally demonstrate that the Bottoms area is vital. Roughly a third of all shorebirds counted at 285 U.S. sites east of the Rockies during the spring were seen at the Bottoms; in autumn, the number was approximately one-quarter of the total shorebirds observed at 510 sites.

The importance of the Bottoms is crucial; a significant percentage of the world populations of stilt and white-rumped sandpipers stop here in spring, with stilt sandpipers stopping in autumn as well. In the case of semipalmated sandpipers, the area is critical to those that pass through on their way to breed on the Alaskan North Slope but is little used by those that breed to the east, as in Canada's Keewatin District. A third group of semipalmated sandpipers that breed in the central Canadian Arctic rely on the Bottoms in the spring but use such Atlantic staging areas as the Bay of Fundy in the autumn. In the case of long-billed dowitchers, the picture is fuzzy: because they regularly, plentifully migrate through areas west of the 105th Meridian, the International Shorebird Survey has not been well established, we can not judge whether their numbers at the Bottoms are a critical proportion of their total population.

While many of these different shorebird species feed on the same foods at Cheyenne Bottoms, they do not necessarily catch their prey in the same spots or by the same methods. According to my friend Wayne Hoffman, who worked with the Kansas Biological Survey, the shorebird habitats can be classified in seven types, including five in the wetlands and two in the uplands.

SHOREBIRD USE OF HABITATS AT CHEYENNE BOTTOMS

Habitat	Number of Species Using as Primary Feeding Habitat	Number of Species Using as Secondary Feeding Habitat
Open water	3	1
Open shallows	12	17
Vegetated shallows	4	6
Open mud	15	5
Vegetated mud	1	3
Open upland	1	1
Vegetated upland	3	1

As shown in the table, the essential appeal of the Bottoms to shorebirds lies with the wetlands. Similarly, Martinez found that only 1.5 percent of the shorebirds he observed were feeding in the uplands, a statistic all the more striking when we consider that about two-thirds of Cheyenne Bottoms is upland.

Given the powerful attraction of the Cheyenne Bottoms wetlands as a biological magnet, its rich invertebrate population enticing such a myriad of birds by providing the nourishment they need to complete their extended migrations, we can only wonder at the consequences if it were destroyed or greatly diminished. Certainly, from the biological point of view, it would seem a risky evolutionary strategy for so many shorebirds to have so many eggs, as it were, in one basket. Here the hand of humankind has played a determining role.

Accounts from market-hunting days, when curlews and other shorebirds were gunned from flocks "darkening the skies" (as described by naturalists of the day), show that the birds were once spread over an enormous expanse of the prairie zone. But the prairies of those days are not the prairies of today: indeed, true natural prairie, dotted in spring with wildflowers and mixed grasses and characterized by sloughs and "sky ponds," has long since been lost to the plow in the American Midwest. A vast stretch of grassland dotted with wetlands well suited to shorebirds has dwindled to a landscape where they can satisfy their needs at just a few rich locations. The consequence, apparently, is that in some years, as when water levels are low, entire shorebird populations are now dependent upon this small number of places for survival.

The shrinking of mixed-grass prairie regions is instructive to conservationists. Beginning during the early 1800s, the impact of expanding human settlement and technological innovation brought rapid, disruptive change to a continental ecosystem that had taken hundreds of thousands of years to develop. In 1837 the introduction of John Deere's steel plow accelerated the tilling of the soil. By the middle of the century, railroad lines from the east had penetrated into Missouri and Kansas, stimulating the demand for agricultural goods and market game for the next thirty years. The rich prairie habitats, including the wetlands, were converted to agricultural production at an enormous rate, a trend that has continued into recent decades.

In Kansas the wetlands have disappeared more quickly than anywhere else. Of the state's wetlands accounted for in a 1955 survey, roughly 40 percent were gone by the next survey, twenty-three years later. As the largest Kansas wetland, Cheyenne Bottoms represents 16 percent of the total remaining. Indeed, the Bottoms has become an oasis for wildlife in a county where 98 percent of the land is dedicated to agriculture.

Today, the quantity of water sufficient to maintain the area is often not available, even though the management still has legal rights to water from the nearby Arkansas River. Thanks to sophisticated developments in pumping technology, the underlying Ogallala Aquifer has been tapped to the point that its upper levels have fallen at some sites by as much as ten feet a year, dramatically lowering the water table and reducing the flow of feeder creeks and streams. Indeed, the Arkansas River's flow has slowed to a mere trickle during much of the year.

This shortage has been particularly problematic for Cheyenne Bottoms, which has not historically been permanent wetland; therefore managers must be able to bring the needed water into play whenever necessary. This situation is complicated not only by the dwindling water resources but also because the annual rainfall is highly variable and has been declining over the past fifty years. Consequently, the problem of diminished water supplies turned into three related problems: an inadequate supply of water, inadequate capabilities for moving available water between the impoundments of the management, and the rapid spread of emergent vegetation, especially narrow-leveled cattail, that was previously controlled by flooding.

Happily, there has been substantial progress in recent years. Thanks to politicking by a good combination of concerned citizens and experts, strengthened by an enormous body of scientific fact collected by conservationists, the Kansas legislature in 1985 commissioned a study of a variety of the complex issues at the Bottoms. One proposed remedy, a rather elaborate network of new and larger dikes, along with new channel and pumping systems for moving water between areas, is now in place.

It remains to be seen whether this project will meet the needs of shorebirds, but they were weighed as an important factor in its design and in implementation of its management scheme. In this case, which could be considered a model for conservationists, the fusion of dedicated, well-executed political action with a mass of solid information led to serious consideration of an environmental problem that in turn resulted in action.

Cheyenne Bottoms is important not only as a singularly rich resource for shorebirds—in a sense, a food oasis—but as a representative example of other sites that act as essential links in the bird-migration chains that connect the opposite ends of our hemispheres. Ensuring that all such

sites are protected will spread the risks of management over the broad-
est possible geographic scale.

Moreover, many sites play more than one role in the sustenance
of species. At the Bottoms, for example, some birds, including snowy
plovers, killdeer, marbled godwits, and American avocets, do not merely
pause but settle in for the summer and nest. Their journey is over, and
the area continues to provide an increasingly scarce resource they need
for feeding and nurturing their next generations, even as the more
ambitious migrants—like Baird's sandpipers, white-rumped sandpipers, and Hudsonian godwits—wing off to their nesting areas on the
northern Canadian tundra and the red knots to the east depart from
Delaware Bay.

Notes

NOTE I

Visual hunters seem to rely on movement to detect and target their prey. In his classic study of redshanks in Scotland, John Goss-Custard found that they feed mostly upon a spry, quick-moving small crustacean, *Corophium volutator*, even when much larger numbers of another favorite prey, a slower-moving polychaete worm, are nearby. He guessed that the redshank spies out *Corophium* more easily because it moves about so rapidly. New evidence indicates that birds have good color vision, but the extent shorebirds employ use of color in foraging is little understood; it seems unlikely that they use color as an important cue in their foraging, since most of their prey is cryptically or dully colored, living out of sight under soft terrain.

There are, by the way, exceptions to the rule that sandpipers generally do not use vision to hunt; indeed, two North American species, the upland and buff-breasted sandpipers, hunt almost exclusively by sight. Because they tend to stand up straighter than other sandpipers, they are better able to spy out insects and other small prey either on or above the ground. Sandpipers like the yellowlegs and spotted sandpipers are also predominantly visual foragers year-round, specializing on prey that live in or around standing water. Only occasionally do they hunt by probing.

Even the sandpipers that usually depend upon touch and "taste" will use their eyesight when it makes more sense, particularly during breeding season. The long-billed curlew forages visually for insects in its thinly grassed nesting habitats, although in winter it probes deep into sand and mud flats for burrowing crustaceans. Another curlew, the whimbrel, also uses sight to find berries and insects in the arctic breeding grounds, only rarely digging into the ground for food. These birds switch to visual cues in summer is all the more interesting since their long decurved bills seem to have evolved specifically to probe efficiently for burrowing prey—especially fiddler crabs—in their wintering areas and along migration routes.

And quite a few other sandpipers well adapted for probing will *occasionally* use eyesight, even when their burrowing prey are abundant. During migration stopovers in Massachusetts, for example, the small sandpipers that typically probe on the intertidal flats uncovered during low tides will switch to visual hunting during high tides, seeking out surface prey on the beachfront or among the tidal wrack.

Other shorebirds will hunt in a variety of ways, such as forcing the bill into the substrate in order to detect prey by touch, by vibrations, or even by chemical cues. In the first category, perhaps the most interesting examples are the long-billed species of sandpipers, including curlews. Their bills have a well-developed system of specialized nerve receptors, known as Herbst's corpuscles, that are thought to recognize prey by touch. Using these sensitive bills, the birds are able to find earthworms in the ground or bivalves—cockles, for example—in marine areas. In much the same way, many smaller probing sandpipers have a slightly enlarged tip to their bills, an area where Herbst's corpuscles are concentrated into a so-called bill-tip organ.

In Holland scientists recently found that some sandpipers that probe into the substrate with their bills partly open are using chemoreception to locate food down in the sand or mud. It turned out that the bills of three different kinds of sandpipers had taste buds concentrated near the top on the inside of the upper and lower bill halves. These sense organs are exposed when the birds forage.

But for knots the story is turning out differently; it is clear that they do not use chemoreception. Nevertheless, another team of Dutch scientists observed that knots were foraging in places on the Wadden Sea coast where, in theory, the prey were so sparsely distributed that knots would be unable to meet their energetic requirements if they were finding prey simply by touch while probing. To explore the matter further, they brought some live knots into captivity and carefully

watched how the knots found arrays of small clams that the researchers had carefully placed and buried in an experimental mud flat. One surprising outcome was that the knots were finding deeply buried prey faster than would be predicted if they were locating them simply by touch. This discovery has prompted the researchers to suggest that the knots can somehow detect the clams through some sense that "reads" changes of "pressure waves" created by the bill probing motion and bounced back from the clam shell to a sense organ in the bird's bill.

NOTE 2

There are two major categories of shorebird feathers: flight and body feathers. The first type, because of the forces encountered during flight, is flexible enough so that wing strokes can simultaneously produce both the equivalent of an aircraft propeller's pitch and the forces of lift. In terms of weight and size, these flight feathers are stronger than any human-made equivalent. Extending from both sides of the outer two-thirds of a central shaft, or quill, are hundreds of barbs. Clasped together by a series of minuscule barbules with hooks that work something like Velcro, the webbed network of barbs forms a flat surface structure known as the vane, the sturdy working area that is found on all flight feathers. These specialized feathers include the inner, or secondary, wing feathers, the outer, or primary, wing feathers, and the shorebird's large tail feathers, called rectrices.

All remaining feathers are body feathers. Some are vaned like flight feathers, including the visible feathers on the bird's back, head, neck, breast, and belly; other feathers are concealed, such as down and the semiplume feathers usually located between the skin and flight feathers, and do not have the structural strength of vanes. These hidden feathers have become adapted to retain the shorebird's body heat and/or to repel water.

Feathers are made of the same keratin proteins as the hair and nails of humans and other mammals, but the similarity ends there. Unlike our fingernails, for instance, the feather does not grow continuously from its base. The reason: the specialized shape of each feather must remain constant for feathers and bird to function properly; if feathers were always growing, the individual feather's shape and corrective relative position would be in constant flux, making it impossible to sustain an efficient airfoil.

NOTE 3

Our work routines at this site generally called for us to hike to one of two areas in search of foraging knots, each about two miles in opposite directions from our base camp. Typically we followed the cliff tops westward to Flechero Bay or eastward to Frecasso and Sarmiento bays. On

more than one occasion, however, we would arrive at one area only to discover that our subjects had flown off in the other direction. This made for some beautiful and exhilarating coastal hikes, sometimes with seabirds virtually alongside us when they were blown close to shore by the Chubut winds. On the other hand, our work was slowed considerably and became especially frustrating when we were loaded down with equipment for catching birds.

We were saved by the arrival of Graham Harris, caretaker of the base camp, which is operated by the New York Zoological Society as a research station. Graham directed us to a small road that wound down to Flechero Bay; after two weeks there, we were finally able to catch some specimens. Our very fine reward was to catch two birds we had banded in Massachusetts some nine months before.

NOTE 4

Incredibly, this extraordinary convocation, one of the world's great ornithological spectacles, took place from time immemorial without any natural historian's knowing about it until quite recently. Even as late as 1937, Delaware Bay naturalist Whitmer Stone made no mention in *Bird Studies at Old May* of the enormous flocks of shorebirds that for weeks routinely commute back and forth between the horseshoe-crab nests on the bay shore and their nighttime resting spots in the adjacent Atlantic marshes. One reason might be, as Stone notes, that it was very difficult to reach these areas before the advent of the automobile, but he does make a suggestive comment without following through on its implications:

> *Walker Hand . . . quotes an old tradition of a regular flight back and forth across the Cape May Peninsula to feed on king [horseshoe] crabs . . .*

Not so long before, in 1934, Julian Potter sent a similarly provocative observation to *Bird Lore*, at that time the journal of the National Audubon Society:

> *Thousands of shore-birds were also reported from the Delaware Bay shore on the 20th [of May]. According to native reports, they were attracted by the king crab spawn on which they were feeding.*

But these very slight hints stand virtually alone, suggesting only that no one yet recognized the fact or the significance of the Delaware Bay layover. This being the case, perhaps it is not entirely inexcusable that in the spring of 1980 I approached the area for the first time with strong doubts about the accuracy of a vague verbal account that "hundreds, maybe thousands" of red knots could be observed there under the full moon of late May. Certainly, I was not prepared to see beaches literally carpeted with tens of thousands of shorebirds, each one alternately shoving its neighbors out of the way and gobbling up horseshoe-crab eggs with furious intensity.

NOTE 5

In science we verify our conclusions with data files and statistical tests, but such verification can take years to establish, especially in the case of slow, sublethal effects. Unfortunately, the manager of an area needs to have credible information in hand before taking action, especially when the associated costs may be high.

Consider oil pollution. The immediate consequences of an accident are vivid—we see oil-covered birds dying on beaches, for example—and yet, no matter how distressing, such clear-cut effects should not be our principal concern. Long after the drama of the disaster has faded from the front burner of public concern, much more serious repercussions might be developing, but it may take decades of work to collect and assess the kind of information fundamental to deciding how much society should invest to reduce the risks of accidents. Such research is so costly that it is rarely undertaken.

Should shippers be required to use thick, double-hulled tankers? What are the long-term effects of spills on invertebrates and eventually on the animals that eat them? How are fisheries and shellfisheries affected? The few studies that exist suggest that the effects of oil spills can linger in ecosystems for a decade or longer. To date, virtually nothing is known for certain about possible "cascade effects" on populations, including humankind, higher up in the food chain.

Studies of pesticides have yielded some of the best illustrations of long-term consequences of environmental insult, for example, the persistence of pollution at Wheeler National Wildlife Refuge in Alabama. In 1947 a chemical company began manufacturing DDT nearby. The estimated 1.5 million gallons of daily wastewater entered the refuge through a ditch, spilling into Indian Creek and then into the Tennessee River, still within Wheeler's boundaries. In 1965, in an attempt to reduce the level of escaping DDT, a settling pond was dug at the head of the waste ditch. Two years later a new ditch and settling pond were constructed, along with other effluent control devices. In 1970, after numerous environmental organizations announced plans to sue, the company voluntarily ceased producing the pesticide. The plant was torn down in 1972, and attempts were made to treat the site to reduce the hazards of any remaining DDT and its breakdown products, or metabolites, such as DDE. But in 1977 a study found that gross pollution remained. New efforts were mounted, including the costly construction of two hazardous-waste sites. Even so, a 1980 study by the U.S. Army Corps of Engineers estimated that 1.6 million pounds of DDT remained in sediments along 2.4 miles of

the Huntsville Spring Branch within the refuge. Both this creek and Indian Creek meander slowly between banks that intermittently spread out into mud flats, creating ideal wildlife habitat.

Science has not yet measured the effects of DDT on migratory shore-birds, but at Wheeler there have been studies of a number of mammals, waterfowl, and waders like herons. As with other animals that move freely between sites, it is not easy to pinpoint where these subjects spend most of their time and therefore where they are most likely to pick up the pesticides and other chemicals that accumulate in their bodies. Nevertheless, the available circumstantial evidence suggests that contamination of Wheeler's wildlife by DDT and metabolites has been extensive. Many kinds of birds that were once common near the top of the food chain have become rare: cormorants, anhingas, herons, and raptors like red-shouldered hawks and barred owls. In some cases populations began to recover in the late 1970s.

On the other hand, time-lapse sampling of wildlife in 1964 and 1979 showed little change in the gross body burdens of DDT in such animals as rabbits and crows. National surveys of pesticide residues in wildlife begun in 1965 by the U.S. Fish and Wildlife Service found seriously elevated DDT and metabolite residues in waterfowl from Alabama. In 1979 young wood ducks in the Huntsville Spring Branch had residues averaging fifty-eight times higher than the mean residues of specimens ninety miles upstream in the

Tennessee River. Fish caught where Indian Creek flows into the river frequently have DDT levels that exceed the tolerance established by the FDA for human food. Commercial fishing has been banned for years in the area, but recreational fishing continues to be by far the most popular visitor activity at Wheeler Refuge.

Much of this information is familiar and has been extensively deliberated, but two points should be considered fundamental: ecosystems are affected for decades by events that were not even recognized as problems when they occurred, and cleanup costs can be very expensive.

NOTE 6

Keeping disturbance issues in mind, some advice can be given for choosing viewing positions. On the Delaware side of the bay, the best locations are the beaches between the towns of Lewes and Slaughter Beach, especially near the mouth of the Mispillion River at falling or rising tides. Although lively and teeming, the flocks of shorebirds there do not typically build to quite as high a concentration as on the Jersey side. For example, there are likely to be significantly fewer of the larger, more colorful birds, like the red knots, ruddy turnstones, and sanderlings. The numbers of smaller semipalmated and least sandpipers, however, do not differ so greatly between the two shores.

On the New Jersey side of the bay,

flocks are usually visible by dawn on the beaches between Norbury's Landing and Fortescue. Typically birds are far more dispersed at lower than at higher tides. The best spot for viewing is most likely at Reed's Beach, especially when the tide rises in the afternoon, causing the shorebirds to collect on the beach before flying off to the Atlantic marshes to roost for the night. Reed's is a less desirable location on weekends, however, when weekend residents and bird watchers frequently disturb the flocks. As a result, the birds sometimes move, either southward to beaches accessible from the Hand Avenue extension or northward to areas inaccessible except by boat. In the latter case, no one seriously concerned about the continued survival of the red knots and other shorebirds would press on stubbornly across the waters to get a good view; boats intrude into the birds' few remaining refuges from human beings.

Another good spot on the Jersey side is Moore's Beach in Cumberland County, particularly at midday during incoming tides. Public access is available where the road first meets the bay shore, except at the highest tides. A walk of a half mile or a mile south along the beach is always pleasant and can sometimes be very rewarding to the bird watcher. (As is true everywhere, you should avoid trespassing on private property.)

Yet another profitable location is the beach at Fortescue during midday after 20 May until 25 May. At the southernmost parts of the beach accessible by road, large flocks of red knots, turn-stones, and sandpipers can often be found from low to mid tides. But during late afternoon, these flocks typically return further southward along the bay shore to Reed's Beach to join the nightly commute to the marshes.

For a good general overview, remember that the principal migration time for most of the shorebirds at Delaware Bay is between 15 May and 31 May. During the earliest days, most foraging takes place between Norbury's Landing and Reed's Beach, but as the month advances and the breeding horseshoe crabs move their beachheads farther up the bay, more and more of the shorebirds follow along—for example, to Moore's Beach and Fortescue. Then Memorial Day often brings a rapid drop in shorebird numbers, perhaps because of the sudden upsurge in the human population on the beach.

I have set down these detailed directions for optimum viewing of shorebirds because I want others to share in the joy of seeing their extraordinary assumption of the bay. But we must all take special care not to disturb them during this essential refueling stop. The time for completing their preparations before flying the next one thousand miles is brief; chronic disturbance impedes their fattening and grooming to a dangerous extent. Ironically, the better they have fed before being disturbed, the more energy it takes (and wastes) to fly their increased weight away when they are startled.

NOTE 7

In science we tend to describe only those ideas and research that have resolved questions, leaving the enigmas and unanswered questions for later research and clarification. The information gaps in our research can be very curious indeed: to take one example, there is an unexplained discrepancy between the number of shorebirds counted at Delaware Bay during spring migration and the much lower numbers seen in autumn throughout the United States.

Based upon our banding program at Manomet, we have estimated a *Calidris canutus rufa* population of about 150,000, a figure that agrees remarkably well with censuses taken across the country in the spring. By contrast, the International Shorebird Survey (ISS) censuses of south migration during the fall indicate a red-knot population of roughly fifty thousand. This kind of discrepancy is representative of the headaches researchers often encounter. In this case so many different factors could possibly influence the results of our banding program or the ISS censusing that the enigma can not easily be resolved.

One possible explanation is that the red knot, along with turnstones and sanderlings, uses different migration strategies according to season. Perhaps the knot uses unknown staging areas somewhere north of the United States in autumn, then flies directly to South America. Another possibility is that turnover rates differ by season; that is, the numbers of each species may build at a staging site in the spring and then all or most of the birds may depart at about the same time, while in the fall their arrivals and departures may both be scattershot. The total number of birds passing through would be much the same. Unfortunately, it would take a considerable amount of research to ascertain the likelihood of this explanation.

Such puzzles and other unanswered questions about the knot do not detract from the basic message of this book, however: because shorebirds are known to concentrate in a relatively small number of migration-staging areas, their populations are extremely vulnerable to loss of those strategic sites. In other words, the conservation issue is clear, even if some of the scientific data are not.

NOTE 8

To estimate the flight-range capability of birds, we use formulas to estimate how much fat a knot of a given size and weight is carrying. If we then assume that the knot will travel at the most efficient altitude and speed, we can estimate how far it is capable of flying. After capturing, weighing, and carefully measuring hundreds of knots, we have concluded that many were quite capable of flying nonstop to South America. This is particularly true of the birds sampled between 27 July and 10 August. After the peak of migration in early August, however, both the remaining adults and the late-arriving juveniles tend

to weigh less on the average, suggesting that few of them would be able to fly directly to a landfall in the Southern Hemisphere.

NOTE 9

In a classic example of long-distance, nonstop migration flight recorded in 1935, a lesser yellowlegs was banded on Cape Cod, then recovered just six days later on Martinique in the Lesser Antilles, a distance of nineteen hundred miles. This recovery was among the earliest and best direct evidence that birds were in fact flying between the northeastern United States and the Caribbean. In the years since, a variety of shorebirds banded during south migration in New England and eastern Canada have been spotted, captured, or shot by locals hunting for food in the countries of northeastern South America and the Caribbean basin. (Unfortunately, such "sportsmen" as recreational gunners on Barbados do not share information about the marked birds they bring down, apparently to hide the total numbers of birds they actually kill.)

One of the most amazing flights ever recorded took place during the summer of 1980, when a semipalmated sandpiper banded in Maine was recovered only two days later in Guyana. Its minimum average ground speed must have exceeded forty miles per hour, making this the fastest flight record yet documented for any shore-bird traveling between North and South America. Even more amazing is that the bird weighed only twenty-seven grams when banded; in other words, it was carrying considerably less fat than theory suggests is required for a trip this long.

In yet another spectacular flight, a ruddy turnstone banded on Saint George Island, Alaska, during the south migration was recovered three-and-one-half days later about twenty-five hundred miles away at French Frigate Shoals in the Hawaiian Leeward Islands. Assuming the unlikely scenario that the bird departed immediately after being marked and was recovered immediately after it landed, it would have flown at a minimum speed of thirty miles per hour for eighty-four hours.

Those who have read this book have learned that my work on knots is part of a team effort that has been touched in hundreds of ways by hundreds of people, so I want to begin this section of thanks with another story. In 1981 our tracking of knots took us to Argentina. We had been preparing for months and believed that all details had been attended to. This was a miserable time in Argentina's history that many people would like to forget, and it clearly was not a time when any sensible person would try to arrange to bring explosives into a country in such turmoil, especially when it was claimed that they would be used to propel a net for catching birds! Somehow, with letters from various governmental authorities, I naively thought all would go well and quickly.

Bill Brewster, Manomet's chairman, had arranged for our banking needs through the Banco de Boston in Buenos Aires. While talking to a man named Charles Rowe, Linda Leddy and I casually mentioned that we needed to get our equipment out of customs. Sr. Rowe, whom we had just met, showed increasing interest in our equipment as we described our list. As I recall, he laughed out loud on mention of the explosives, walked over to his phone, and called in Sr. Eduardo Giacinto. Mr. Rowe and Mr. Giacinto knew well that expert assistance was going to be needed to retrieve our equipment from customs. Although Mr. Giacinto was the customs expert for the bank, it took every hour of his next three days, and hundreds of miles of rushing from one office to another—some downtown, others at the the far-away airport—to negotiate arrangements and to collect dozens of correctly colored ink stamps marked with indecipherable signatures and initials. On the last morning (a Saturday I think) we were already late in leaving Buenos Aires to meet our team that would soon be arriving by air in Trelew, a city 850 miles south. At last, the final piece of paper was secured shortly before offices closed. Sr. Giacinto rushed to the airport to assist with the final step: inspection of our huge wooden crate, far too big to get into our overpacked, small sedan. We hastily unloaded the nets, explosives, and other equipment into the car trunk and asked Mr. Giacinto how we could repay him for his help. He would accept nothing until he saw that we would not be taking the wooden crate. Our last view of him was heading back towards Buenos Aires in his small gray car with a huge wooden crate strapped to the roof. There is no question that his help prevented total failure of the expedition and the loss of thousands of dollars in equipment, time, and travel. We had not asked for help, but he and Mr. Rowe had seen the need and given it. Our journeys and work have been sustained by this kind of spirit dozens of times in virtually every country where we have followed knots. Naming every appropriate person and instance would double the cost of this book. I am comfortable thinking that some reward to all these friends will come through having contributed to learning more about shorebirds' tenuous global lifestyle, which is leading to protection and management measures needed for the small number of places that are so critical to them. Thank you.

Among the hundreds of people who have been members of field expeditions or who have otherwise helped us in our programs are trustees, councillors, and special friends of Manomet Observatory, students in the Manomet Field Biology training program, and associates from the governmental and nongovernmental agencies in the countries where we have worked. We have hiked in mud to our knees, slept in leaking tents, greeted scorpions in our shoes and found many other exclamation points punctuating adventures with wonderful people from Argentina, Uruguay, Brazil, Surinam, Venezuela, Chile, Peru, Ecuador, Colombia, the United States, Canada, Sweden, the United Kingdom, and the Netherlands. We owe special thanks to wildlife and other governmental agencies in Argentina, Brazil, Surinam, Venezuela, the United States—especially the U.S. Fish and Wildlife Service, and the Canadian Wildlife Service. Financial support also has come from a long roster of people and organizations listed at the end of this section. I fully anticipate some feelings of disappointment when I learn whom I have left off this list, and I apologize for those inadvertent errors.

There is always a risk of singling out individuals for special mention when so many hundreds of people have been involved. I need to resist a long proclamation of thanks to my family who have tolerated my long absences, sometimes without communication for weeks on end; the few trips we have shared have been wonderful—the rest wonderful too, but with a missing element. The knots, their habitats, and my work have been given pivotal financial and program support by Mr. and Mrs. William S. Brewster, Mrs. Nancy A. Claflin, Mr. and Mrs. Theodore L. Cross, Mr. and Mrs. John Fiske, Mr. and Mrs. John C. Fuller, Mr. and Mrs. Edwin F. Gamble, Mr. John Hay, Mr. and Mrs. Weston Howland, Jr., Mr. and Mrs. John F. Hubbard, Mr. and Mrs. Henry Lyman, Mr. and Mrs. August R. Meyer, Mrs. Louville F. Niles, Mr. and Mrs. Edward H. Raymond, Mr. and Mrs. Peter M. Richards, and Mr. and Mrs. Jeptha H. Wade. Foundation and organizational support has been given by The Geraldine R. Dodge Foundation, The William H. Donner Foundation, The Richard King Mellon Foundation, The William P. Wharton Trust, Birdlife International (formerly The International Council for Bird Preservation), The U.S. Fish and Wildlife Service, The World Wildlife Fund—U.S., and by anonymous donors. Thanks to all.

Preparing this book has required the undeserved patience of Jim Mairs, editor at W. W. Norton & Company. The idea developed soon after NOVA, the PBS television series produced by WGBH Educational Foundation, selected red knots for a feature about migration. Working with Nancy Lattanzio, senior editor at WGBH and writer Charles Flowers has been a pleasant, rewarding, and educational journey of its own; without their skills and encouragement we would have a Gordian knot rather than a bookish knot. Others at WGBH who helped in various ways include Jeffrey Rothenberg, William Scheller, Karen Johnson, Doug Scott, Mary Cahill, and Paula Apsell, NOVA's executive producer. A number of photographers have given us advice as well as opportunities to use their work at no cost or at below market rates. We have enjoyed scanning through hundreds of your photographs. Thank you Fred Bruemmer, Pablo Canevari, Theodore Cross, Arthur Morris, Dave Twichell, and folks at the Wildlife Collection. Finally, the manuscript has benefited from the very helpful critiques given by Guy Morrison of the Canadian Wildlife Service, Theunis Piersma of the

Netherlands Institute for Sea Research, and Chris Leahy of the Massachusetts Audubon Society.

Many of the photographs were taken by David C. Twichell. Dave has traveled with us from Tierra del Fuego to James Bay, always lugging camera equipment, sometimes hiking over rugged terrain for miles on end, sometimes stuffed into tiny seats as we flew dangerously low over Atlantic coastlines in search of knots. We have shared wonderful as well as difficult times. I name Dave because he is a great friend, but more because he is one of those people who shared a dream and was instrumental in making it happen. For the same reason, I want to thank other friends: Kathleen Anderson, director emeritus; Linda Leddy, president; and William Brewster, former chairman of the board of Manomet Observatory, which has employed me for more than two decades.

Finally, I want to note that my early years of work with knots were frequently guided by advice from the late Joseph A. Hagar. Through years of travel and skilled field observation, "Archie" developed rare insights into knots' life cycles, especially during their migrations. He understood why this was the "right bird" to carry the natural history and conservation message that needed telling. This book testifies to the exactitude of Archie's "hunches," and to the work of uncounted numbers of people who translated his advice into the natural history knowledge so essential to prudent conservation planning.

NOVA is made possible by grants from Merck & Company, Inc., Raytheon Company, the Corporation for Public Broadcasting, and public television viewers.

Index

Page numbers in *italics* refer to illustrations.

Alaska, 118, 142, 163
albatross, 109
Alerstam, Thomas, 166–67
American avocet, 170, 175
American Birds, 150
American oystercatcher, 57, 146
American woodcock, 146
amphipods, 105
anhinga, 180*n*
Antarctica, 13
arctic fox, 89–91
Argentina, 9, 20, *24,* 36, 40, 61,
    113–15, *131,* 137
Army Corps of Engineers, 180*n*
Audubon, 160
Audubon, John James, 141, 148, 149,
    150
Audubon Society:
    National, 179*n*
    New Jersey, 124
Australia, 30, 118
avocet, American, 170, 175

Bahia Bustamente, Argentina, 37
Bahia San Sebastian, Argentina, 37, 47
Baird's sandpiper, 169, 170, 175
banding, *24, 25,* 107–8, 183*n*
    site fidelity and, 141–44
Barbados, 183*n*
barred owl, 180*n*
Bay of Fundy, 16, 122, 155, 171
    hydroelectric development and,
        123–24
beach fleas, 105
Bird Lore, 179*n*
Bird Studies at Old May (Stone),
    178*n*–79*n*
black-bellied plover, 9, 92, 100, 128,
    131, 155
black turnstone, 120, 121
Brazil, 6, 16, 20, 53–54, 56, 60–61, 65,
    137
breeding:
    courtship display and, 88

egg clutch and, 88–89
feigning injury ploy and, 88–91, 93
incubation and, 89
leks and, 93
migration's effect on, 91
nests and, 88–91
patterns of, 91–94
polyandry and, 92–93
predation and, 93–94
promiscuity and, 93
serial polygyny and, 92–93
buff-breasted sandpiper, 93, 176*n*

Calidris canutus rufa, see red knot
California, 17
Canada, 115, 118, 136, 138–39, 155,
    156, 163, 171
    hydroelectric projects of, 122–24
Canadian Wildlife Service, 20, 21, 36,
    110, 124
Canevari, Pablo, 37
Cape Cod, Mass., 102–4, *107,* 183*n*
Cape Henlopen, Del., 65
Cape May, N.J., 65, 76
Cape May Bird Observatory, 124
Cape May National Wildlife Refuge,
    125
chemoreception, 146, 177*n*
Cheyenne Bottoms, Kans., 16, 25,
    169–72
    human intrusion and, 172–74
    importance of, 171, 174–75
    prairie habitat and, 173
    shorebird habitat classification at,
        171–72
    water management and, 173–74
Chile, 137–38
chironomid midges, 170, 171
Churchill, Man., 86
clams, 37, *38,* 53, 60, 61, *67, 150,* 161
Clean Water Act (1977), 153
Coast Guard, 153
Cobb's Island, Va., 64
cochina clam (donax), *38,* 60, *67, 150*
Connecticut, 160
conservation, 24
    chain of reserves and, 136–37
    of Cheyenne Bottoms, 173–74
    of Delaware Bay, 124–28
    education and, 125, *126*

international cooperation and,
    132–39
of Jamaica Bay, 128–32
network approach to, 137–39
oil pollution and, 179*n*–80*n*
pesticides and, 180*n*
research and, 24–25
conservative mating pattern, 91–92
Coolidge, Herman, 64
copepod, 170
coquina clams, 61
Corophium amphoid, 124, 176*n*
coscoroba swan, *131*
courtship display, 88
crab, horseshoe, *see* horseshoe crab
curlews:
    Eskimo, 149
    long-billed, 176*n*
curlew sandpiper, 93

DDT, 180*n*–81*n*
Delaware Bay, 6, 20, 25, 61, *158,* 163,
    169
    conservation of, 124–28
    current threats to, 152–57
    importance of, 155
    migration approach to, 64–67
    migration departure from, 84–85
    migration spectacle in, 8, 73–75, 77
    migration time at, 182*n*
    viewing positions at, 181*n*–82*n*
Delaware coastal management
    program, 125–28
Delaware Fish and Wildlife, 125
Delaware Nature Society, 125
Delaware Shorebird Protection
    Committee, 125
Delaware Wild Lands, Inc., 125
Delmarva peninsula, 64
detritivores, 161
donax (cochina clams), *38,* 60, *67, 150*
dowitchers:
    long-billed, 118–20, 170, 171
    short-billed, 88, 110, 112, 118–20
"dread" flight, *82,* 84–85
duck, wood, 180*n*
dunlin, 45, 73, 92, 100, 101, 118
Dutch Guiana, *see* Surinam
"dynamic soaring," 109

190   eastern phoebe, 141
eggs, 88–89, 91
Environmental Protection Agency
  (EPA), 153
Eskimo curlew, 149
Europe, 52
Exxon Valdez disaster, 120–22, 153

falcons, 41, *58*
  peregrine, 44–45
feathers:
  categories of, 177n–78n
  molting of, 45–47
Fish and Wildlife Agency, 153
Fish and Wildlife Service, 128, 180n
fleas, beach, 105
flight:
  "dread," *82*, 84–85
  "dynamic soaring," 109
  fat reserves and, 110
  formation, 37–45
  predators and, 40–44
  resting sites and, 38–40
  speed and, 109–10
  wing shape and, 108–9, 110
Florida, *14, 20, 107,* 108
food, foraging, 33, 36–37, 60
  active prey and, 145
  competition for, 146
  conservation and, 147
  foraging methods and, 176n–77n
  foraging zones and, 101
  Guiana coast and, 112–13
  horseshoe crab spawning and,
    73–77
  in James Bay, 100–101
  length of day and, 52
  population size and, 146
  prey movement and, 176n
  resting sites and, 38–40, 178n–79n
  salinity and, 101–2, 123
  sedentary prey and, 145–46
  sodbank habitat and, 104–5
  tidal flux and, 52, 53
  visual hunting and, 176n
  weight and, 52
Food and Drug Administration
  (FDA), 181n
Forbush, E. H., 150

Forsythe National Wildlife Refuge,
  105
Fortescue, N.J., 84, 181n–82n
fox, arctic, 89–91
French Guiana, 110

Game Birds, Wild-Fowl and Shorebirds
  (Forbush), 150
Gateway National Recreation Area,
  131
gem clams, 161
Georgia, 61
global warming, 154–55
godwits:
  Hudsonian, 57, 88, 92, 100, 171, 175
  marbled, 100, 175
golden plover, *see* lesser golden plover
Golfo San Jorge, Argentina, *34,* 40,
  53, *58*
goshawk, 109
Goss-Custard, John, 176n
Grande Complex, La, 122–23
great black-backed gull, *78*
Great Egg Harbor, N.J., 105
greater yellowlegs, 100, 110, 112, 145,
  176n
gulls, 73
  great black-backed, *78*
  herring, 78
  laughing, *46, 78*
Guyana, 108, 110, 113, 183n

Hagar, Joseph, 86
Hand, Walker, 179n
Harris, Graham, 178n
Haustorius, 105
hawk, red-shouldered, 109, 180n
Herbst's corpuscles, 177n
herring, 120–21
herring gull, *78*
Hoffman, Wayne, 171–72
homing pigeons, 166
horseshoe crab *(Limulus polyphemus),*
  67, 70–77, *78,* 84, 110, 153, 157,
  158, 182n
  global warming and, 154
  migration of, 72, 154
  spawning by, 72–76
  tides and, 77
Hudson Bay, 85, 100, 123

Hudsonian godwit, 57, 88, 92, 100,
  171, 175
hydroelectric development, 122–24

International Shorebird Survey
  (ISS), 24, 25, 124, 136, 150, 170,
  171, 182n
intertidal mudflats, 101
Iowa, 17

Jamaica Bay Wildlife Refuge, 128–32
James Bay, Canada, 16, 20, 85, *98,* 108,
  156–57
  fecundity of, 100–102
  hydroelectric development of, 122
Johnsson, Lars, 89
Johnston Atoll, 9

Kansas, 156, 169, 173–74
Kansas Biological Survey, 171
keratin, 178n
killdeer, 86, 169, 175
knot, red, *see* red knot

Lagoa do Peixe, Brazil, 25, 41, 44, 54,
  56–61, 137
laughing gull, *46, 78*
Laysan Island, 141–42
least sandpiper, 100, 181n
Leddy, Linda, 110
leks, 93
Leopold, Aldo, 169
lesser golden plover, 9, 86, 88, 100,
  120, 141–42
  market hunting of, 148–50
lesser yellowlegs, 86, 100, 101, 110,
  112, 145, 170, 176n, 183n
Lester, Robert T., 153
Limulus polyphemus, see horseshoe crab
long-billed curlew, 176n
long-billed dowitcher, 118–20, 170,
  171

Macoma balthica, 100, 101
magnetism, *115,* 164–66
Manomet Observatory, 21, 64, 86,
  136, 182n
marbled godwit, 100, 175
Maritimes Shorebird Survey, 136
market hunting, 148–50

Martinez, Ed, 170–71, 172
Martini, Peter, 101
Martinique, 183*n*
Mary's Point, N.B., 124
Massachusetts, 9, 20, 76, 102–5,
    107–8, 110, 124, 142–44, 146–47,
    163
Metropolitan Transit Authority, N.Y.,
    129
Mexico, 137, 138–39
midges, chironomid, 170, 171
migration, 9
    altitude and, 109–11
    breeding affected by, 91
    caloric consumption and, 54
    censusing efforts and, 20–21
    Cheyenne Bottoms and, 169–70
    departure from stopovers and,
        84–85
    Exxon Valdez disaster and, 120–21
    fat reserves and, 53–54, 56–57
    first-time, 167–68
    flight speed and, 109–11
    food availability and, 33
    global warming and, 154–55
    of horseshoe crabs, 72, 154
    hydroelectric developments and,
        122–24
    length of day and, 37, 54
    long-distance non-stop, 183*n*–84*n*
    magnetism and, 164–66
    molt and, 47
    navigation and, *see* navigation
    nomadicism and, 32–33
    nonmarine sites and, 156
    polarized light and, *115*, 164, 166
    research and, 21–25
    site fidelity and, 141–44
    from southern Brazil to U.S., 61–65
    spring vs. fall, 155–56
    traditional staging areas and, 12, 16
    weather and, 65–67, 166–67
    wing shape and, 108–9, 110
Missouri, 17, 173
molting, 45–47
Monomoy Wilderness Area, 104, *134*
Montague Island, Alaska, 120, 121
Moore's Beach, N.J., 181*n*, 182*n*
Morrison, Guy, 20, 21, 36–37, 101,
    110

Moses, Robert, 129, 132
mud:
    biological productivity of, 160–62
    grain size and, 162
    "sling," 112
mudflats, intertidal, 101
mussel spat, 33, 36, 104, *107*, 110,
    144, 146
Myers, J. P., 153

National Audubon Society, 179*n*
National Oceanic and Atmospheric
    Agency, 153
National Park Service, 128, 131
Natural Lands Trust, 125
Natural Resources and Environmen-
    tal Control Department, Delaware,
    124, 125
Nature Conservancy, 125
Nauset Beach, Mass., 102–4
navigation, *115*, 163–68
    by juvenile birds, 167–68
    magnetic polarity and, 164–66
    radar studies of, 163
    weather and, 167–68
nests, *86*, 88
    predation and, 89–91
New Jersey, 6–8, 70
New Jersey Audubon Society, 124
New Jersey Conservation
    Foundation, 125
New Jersey Fish and Wildlife, 124, 125
New Jersey Power and Light
    Company, 125
New York Zoological Society, 178*n*
New Zealand, 30
Northwest Territories, 85

Office of Technology Assessment, 17
Ontario, 100
opportunistic mating pattern, 91–92
owl, barred, 180*n*
oystercatcher, American, 57, 146

"paper parks," 137
Parks Department, N.Y., 129
Patagonia, 32, 37, 52, *67*, 110, 115
    restinga of, 33, *34*, 36–37, 38, 52, 104
Payne, Laura, 115
pectoral sandpiper, 93, 142, 171

Peninsula Valdez, Argentina, 52–53,
    54, 56
peregrine falcon, 44–45
Peru, 137, 138
phalarope, Wilson's, 170
philopatry (site fidelity), 141–44
phoebe, eastern, 141
Piersma, Theunis, 89–91
pigeons, homing, 166
Pleske, Theodore, 88–89
plovers:
    black-bellied, 9, 92, 100, 128, 131,
        155
    lesser golden, 9, 86, 88, 100, 120,
        141–42, 148–50
    semipalmated, 88, 100, 110, 112
    snowy, 175
plumage, *10*, *14*, *30*, 77, *78*, *91*, 93, 94,
    102
Plum Island, Mass., 104
Plymouth Beach, Mass., 102, 105, *118*,
    144
polarized light, *115*, 164, 166
polyandry, 92–93
polychaete worms, 53, 146, 176*n*
Potter, Julian, 179*n*
predators, predation, 40–41
    breeding and, 93–94
    family groupings and, 91
    formation flying and, 41–44
    nests and, 89–91
    reaction of knots to, 93–94
    rest sites and, 105–7
preening, 40, 46, 105
Prince William Sound, 118–21

Quebec, 100, 123

red knot (*Calidris canutus rufa*):
    courtship display of, 88
    described, 30
    digestive system of, 36
    distinguishing sex of, 102
    egg clutch of, *86*
    formation flying and, 37–45
    nestlings of, 91, *91*
    nest of, *86*
    nomadic nature of, 32–33
    numbers of, 21, 57, 182*n*

U.S. winter population of, *14, 107,*
108
western, 118–20
wintering grounds of, 30–32, 36–37
red-shouldered hawk, 109, 180*n*
Reed's Beach, N.J., *6,* 73, 76, 181*n,*
182*n*
restinga, 33, *34,* 36–37, 38, 52, 104
rheas, *58*
Rhode Island, 6, 9
Rimmer, Chris, 85
Rio Grande, Argentina, 36, 38, 41
Rio Grande do Sul, Brazil, 56–57, 60,
61, 137
Rocky Bay staging area, 120–121
Ross, Ken, 37, 110
ruddy turnstone, *46,* 57, 70, 73, 76–77,
78, 84–85, 91, 100, 101, 146, 156,
181*n,* 182*n,* 184*n*

Saint George Island, Alaska, 184n
Sand County Almanac, A (Leopold), 169
sanderling, 70, 73, 76–77, 84–85,
100, 156, 181*n,* 182*n*
opportunistic breeding pattern of,
92
sandpipers:
Baird's, 169, 170, 175
buff-breasted, 93, 176*n*
curlew, 93
least, 100, 181*n*
pectoral, 93, 142, 171
semipalmated, *see* semipalmated
sandpiper
sharp-tailed, 93
stilt, 88, 92, 171
upland, 176*n*
western, 92, 118
white-rumped, 93, 110, 171, 175
semipalmated plover, 88, 100, 110,
112
semipalmated sandpiper, 70, 76–77,
86–88, *98,* 100, 101, 110, 112,
155–56, 170, 171, 181*n*
"dread" flights and, 84–85
flight record of, 183*n*–84*n*
numbers of, 21, 73
serial polygyny, 92–93
sharp-tailed sandpiper, 93
shorebirds, 8, 73
bills of, 177*n*

breeding patterns of, 91–93
censusing, 17–21, 24, 110–12
color vision of, 176*n*
conservation of, *see* conservation
diet of, 145–47
fat storage by, 53–54, 56–57
flight speed of, 109–10
foraging patterns of, 36, 52,
176*n*–77*n*
formation flying by, 37–45
habitats classification for, 171–72
human disturbance and, 77–78, 107
market hunting of, 148–50
marking, 20–21, *24*
number of species of, 12
wing shape of, 109
short-billed dowitcher, 88, 110, 112,
118–20
Siberia, 88, 89
site fidelity (philopatry), 141–44
"sling mud," 112
snowy plover, 175
sodbanks, 104–5, *107,* 144
sooty tern, 141
South Africa, 30–32
South Carolina, 61
spat, mussel, 33, 36, 104, *107,* 110,
144, 146
staging areas:
categories of, 136
character of, 16
conservation of, 133–36, 147
of Massachusetts, 102–4
of Prince William Sound, 120–22
sodbank habitat and, 104
suitable features of, 107
wetlands and, 16–17
Steinhart, Peter, 160
stilt sandpiper, 88, 92, 171
Stone, Whitmer, 178*n*–79*n*
Stone Harbor, N.J., 76
surfbirds, 120, 121
Surinam, 16, 108
wintering grounds in, 110–13
swan, coscoroba, *131*
Sweden, 166–67

tanaidae, 112
tellin clams, 37, 53
tern, sooty, 141
Texas, 20, 108

Third Cliff Beach, Mass., *102,* 104
Tierra del Fuego, 8, 32, 33, 36–37,
38, 52, 137
tundra, 86
turnstones:
black, 120, 121
ruddy, *46,* 57, 70, 73, 76–77, *78,*
84–85, 91, 100, 101, 146, 156,
181*n,* 182*n,* 184*n*

United Kingdom, 52, 56
upland sandpiper, 176*n*
Uruguay, 113, 137

Venezuela, 20, 61, 137, 138
Virginia, 64

waders, *see* shorebirds
Wassaw Island, Ga., 64
weather, 65–67, 85, 166–68
Western Hemisphere Shorebird
Proclamation, 125
Western Hemisphere Shorebird
Reserve Network (WHSRN), 25,
113, 124, *131,* 132, 136–39
western sandpiper, 92, 118
wetlands, 13, 137, 154, 172, 173–74
defined, 16
importance of, 16–17
in U.S., 17
Wetlands for the Americas (WA), 25,
136, 138
Wheeler National Wildlife Refuge,
180*n*
whimbrel, 88, 110, 176*n*
white-rumped sandpiper, 93, 110,
171, 175
willet, 110, 112
Wilson's phalarope, 170
wings, 30
shape of, 108–9, 110
woodcock, American, 146
wood duck, 180*n*
World Wildlife Fund, 36
worms, polychaete, 53, 146, 176*n*

yellowlegs:
greater, 100, 110, 112, 145, 176*n*
lesser, 86, 100, 101, 110, 112, 145,
170, 176*n,* 183*n*

DATE DUE

DEC 19 2003			
DEC 13 2004			